FROM SHARECROPPER'S SON TO WHO'S WHO IN AMERICAN WOMEN

A Memoir
By Phoebe Smith

ISBN: 0692244263
ISBN-13: 9780692244265

This book is dedicated with love to my parents,
Eva Thompson Smith and James Cleve Smith

The Marquis Who's Who
Publications Board

Certifies that

Phoebe Smith

is a subject of biographical record in

Who's Who of American Women
Fifteenth Edition
1987/1988

inclusion in which is limited to those individuals who have demonstrated outstanding achievement in their own fields of endeavor and who have, thereby, contributed significantly to the betterment of contemporary society.

President

INTRODUCTION

At two o'clock in the morning of January 31, 1969, I walked across the Mexican border into Tijuana. My purpose – sex-change surgery. This book is an account of the events in my life leading up to that trip to Mexico and afterwards.

It is a compilation of diary entries, letters, remembrances throughout my life and articles I wrote for THE TRANSSEXUAL VOICE which I think are relevant today.

Beginning with my birth and childhood on the farm and, then the excitement of moving to Atlanta when I was fourteen. I was known as a sissy throughout my childhood. When I entered high school, I was called a queer by fellow students.

I never thought I was a homosexual but I was attracted to boys, so what else could I be? I was in my mid-teens when I first heard of sex-change surgery and transsexuals. I knew nothing about the subject, but I was sure I was one.

I spent the remainder of my teens and my twenties searching for information and doctors. I might as well have been a Martian in disguise trying to fit in. It was a terrifying situation. Remember, in the late fifties and throughout the sixties and beyond, the subject of transsexuals or having a sex-change operation was taboo, and in most peoples' mind was impossible and anyone who would mention it was thought to be a pervert.

It was desperation, not nerve that helped me get through the years of struggling to find a solution to my dilemma. A desire to get even with the people who bullied and teased me also helped me keep going. Ending my life would have been far easier than what I endured. Not wanting to hurt my parents is the only reason I didn't take the easy way to end my problem.

All the hell I put myself through dealing with Vocational Rehabilitation and medical professionals could have been avoided if I had known that I would someday achieve my goal with the help of my parents. (They were not always in a position to help me.) Had I not gone through those experiences, my story would have had a very different ending. If I had ever completely given up on reaching my goal, I would have given up on life.

I was twenty-nine years old when I walked across the border into Tijuana.

Age Three

ONE

I come from a family of sharecroppers, and both my mother and father had thirteen siblings. (My maternal grandfather remarried after the death of my grandmother, and that union produced two more children.) We lived on a farm in Irwin County, Georgia, about two hundred miles south of Atlanta. It was there that I was born on October 11th, 1939.

Mother had been born on a farm, so I'm sure she didn't think twice about giving birth to me there. But nothing could have prepared her for what was to come. The first doctor who came to the house couldn't deliver me, and a second doctor was called. I should have been delivered by Cesarean section in a hospital. Both my mother and I were expected to die, but the decision was made to try to save me. The doctor tore me from my mother, leaving her near death and requiring repair surgery. As for me, my neck was stretched and I had indentations on my head from the forceps. I still have one of the indentations.

Mother gave birth to two more sons. Norman was born September of 1941 in Tift County Hospital. I was almost two years old. He went home from the hospital but when he was only six weeks old, he returned to the hospital where he died. No diagnosis was given to my parents.

I was almost five years old when my brother Billy was born in August of 1944. He was born on daddy's birthday. Daddy was born just outside of Atlanta on a dairy farm. When he was a teenager his family moved to Florida, near Orlando. After a few years, they returned to Georgia. They settled on a farm near Tifton, the county seat of Tift County which adjoins Irwin County.

Daddy was five-feet-eleven inches tall, and weighed about one hundred seventy pounds. He was a jovial person. He lost an eye during a baseball game with family and friends when he was about eight years old. Someone accidentally hit him in the eye with a baseball and the eye burst and had to be removed.

Mother was five foot, three inches tall and was quite skinny in the early part of her life. She was very attractive. She was the best cook in her family. That was attributed to the fact that she assisted her mother in the kitchen and her siblings worked on the farm. She was primarily interested in family and church and never worked outside the home.

Ours was a loving home, with plenty of family around. My parents were not argumentative. Our home environment was peaceful and I always felt safe.. My father never made it past the fifth grade, but he was very good with numbers, and could figure something in his head as quickly as I could do it on paper.

My early years were pretty much what you'd expect for someone who grew up on a farm in South Georgia. Even though we were poor, I remember those early years as the happiest years of my life. The complications that were to plague my later years were not yet evident—or at least, not yet identifiable. True, I did prefer playing with girls to boys, and dolls to cowboy guns. And, by the time I started school, relatives were already calling me a sissy.

When I started school, I was in quite a few plays and I even sang a duet in the second grade. I had always been outgoing and liked to be included in any kind of activity. But, my sissy ways did not go unnoticed. This didn't bother me too much the first two or three years. I was accustomed to being called sissy by family.

Mother needed a hysterectomy in 1945. She was admitted to Piedmont Hospital in Atlanta. She was allergic to the sulfa drug they gave her, but her allergy went undetected and they continued to give it to her. She became very ill and lost a lot of weight. The doctors decided she must have cancer and sent her back to Tifton Hospital. I rode along in the ambulance with my mother and grandmother.

I don't remember much about her illness but one of my uncles told me how she screamed in pain. Mother's younger sister Lutrelle, requested that she be transferred to the hospital in Thomasville, Georgia. During exploratory surgery, it was discovered that she had a blocked kidney. In removing her kidney, the surgeons cut her halfway around her body. She weighed seventy-nine pounds when she came home from the hospital.

When I was in the fourth grade, I started a new school because my family had gone to live with my grandfather following the October 1948 death of my grandmother. This was the point in my life when being known as a sissy started making me the target of bullying. I didn't understand my actions, myself, and I certainly couldn't have described my feelings to anyone else. Now I was in a new school, having to contend with bullies. I was always getting my feelings hurt and I began to withdraw from group activity.

During the summer between the fourth and fifth grades I earned a little money working in tobacco. I used some of the money to buy paper dolls. I knew Daddy would not approve so I hid under the bed to play with them. When my father discovered them, he burned them and told me I better not buy any more. But, I did and he burned them too. I didn't buy any more after that because I knew I would get a whipping if I did.

When school began again, I thought things might be better but they weren't. I was now in the fifth grade. Some days, part of the class would go to the library. One particular day, I was among the students selected to go to the library. We were all seated next to each other around a table when one of the boys got a whiff of me. He asked me what I was wearing in a voice loud enough for everyone to hear. That morning before school, I'd gotten into my mother's bath powder and overdid it a bit. I tried to deny it, but it was obvious. I smelled like perfumed talc. By the end of the day everyone knew about it.

About once a month the class had a spelling bee, and the captain of each team would select a player. I was always the last one chosen. I would act silly and laugh, pretending I didn't care, but I did. The sixth grade was just more of the same.

When school was out for the summer of 1951, we moved to Atlanta. I loved it. I got to know my Atlanta relatives much better. We lived just up the street from my grandparents' grocery store, and I spent as much time visiting with them as I could. They carried a few ladies' accessories in the store—things like wallets, scarves, and jewelry. I bought a ladies' wallet and two neck scarves, one pastel pink and the other blue. I had to hide them but, when I was home alone, I took them out and wore them for a few minutes.

Daddy worked for Otis Elevator Company and was only home on the weekends. He didn't like living in Atlanta and did not like being on the road. At the end of 1951, he moved the family back to the farm. I hated it.

When I entered the seventh grade, I had a familiar teacher. She had taught me in the fifth grade at another school in the county. She was not very well liked by the other students, but she took an instant liking to me. It was the only time I was ever known as the teacher's pet. This did nothing to make me popular with the other students. I didn't do myself any favors either. I had such a strong desire to wear my pink and blue neck scarves, I took one of them to school and went into the restroom to put it on.

When the laughing and teasing started, I tried to tell everyone, "In Atlanta, boys wear scarves!" Everyone knew better, of course. Atlanta was only two hundred miles away—not on another planet. I set myself up and the repercussions stayed with me. I was bullied, pushed down, hit in the stomach and I was told I'd better not tell anyone, and I didn't. I don't know who come up with the name, but from then on, I was known as "Sissy Faye."

I was afraid of confrontation. I only felt safe when I was at home. I would do whatever I could to escape the bullying. There were several tall, thick bushes in a circle in the school yard, with a small clearing in the middle. During recess and lunch, I would go into the bushes and hide. I never told my family or anyone else about the bullying. I always shielded my parents from the knowledge of how I was treated. I didn't want them to worry about me.

One day, my mother and I were shopping in a store when we met up with my teacher. While they were talking, I wandered away. Later that night, mother told me that my teacher had told her, "J.C. takes the teasing well." She asked me what the teacher was talking about, but I had no idea exactly what the teacher had told her. So, I said, "Me and two other boys don't play ball with the other boys so they call us sissies." I tried to act as if it was nothing because I didn't want her to worry.

During the summer of 1953, when I was almost fourteen years old, Daddy made me start doing real farm work. He tried to teach me how to milk a cow. I tried to copy what he did, but it didn't work. He thought I was intentionally messing up, but it wasn't true.

One day, he hitched the mule to the weeder and told me that I had to weed a field of peanuts. I was afraid of the mule but I was more afraid that I would find a snake. I have always been terrified of snakes. When I got near the end of the field, I turned the mule around before I got to the end of the peanut row, which was at a fence that was all grown up with weeds. I made such a mess of the end of the peanut rows, I didn't have to do anything with the mule again. I did work in tobacco and picked a little cotton. I hated picking cotton just as much as I hated school.

When my parents visited relatives on Sundays, I stayed home. As soon as they left, I headed for my mother's makeup and sometimes I would put on her dresses. Somehow it was reassuring, and I was always pleased with how I looked. I made sure all traces of makeup were gone before they returned home.

I always assumed I would outgrow my sissy ways as I grew older. I didn't like being called a sissy, but I didn't like being a boy either. At the time, I didn't worry about it. I suppose my young mind allowed me to believe that in time, everything would work itself out.

After Labor Day of 1953, I started high school in Tifton, Georgia. The following Sunday, my entire family was involved in a wreck. The pickup truck in which we were riding was hit by a big flatbed truck. My parents were seriously injured. When I regained consciousness, I was lying on my father, and my mother was lying crumpled over the steering wheel. She was covered with blood, and I thought she was dead. Although my father's left arm was crushed when the truck turned over, he lifted my mother from the wreckage and passed her to someone outside.

I fainted when I was removed from the truck. I heard my mother pleading with my father to take care of my brother and me. She thought she was dying and, for several days, she wasn't expected to live. She had a broken pelvis, a fractured neck, a big gash on her head, and broken teeth. My father's shoulder was broken. My brother Billy had a broken ankle. I had a broken pelvis. I spent two weeks in the hospital and three months in bed at the home of relatives.

It was mid-December before we were home again. My father was unable to farm anymore, and my mother was in constant pain and unable to do anything. Mrs. Spicer, an elderly friend of the family stayed with us for a few weeks.

In early February we moved back to Atlanta. I was so excited to leave the farm, and sure that this time, we were in Atlanta to stay. I entered the ninth grade at Roosevelt High—a huge school. The best thing about going to a new school was that no one would know I had always been called a sissy. Being in Atlanta didn't change who I was, and being myself made me a target of bullying. I thought the bullying would subside as I got older but it actually got worse.

I loved my new school until I learned a new word—"queer." Although I was attracted to boys, I didn't consider myself gay, but my classmates did. I hated the word "queer" even before I knew what it meant; I knew it wasn't a good thing to be called. I'm sure being a countrified sissy made me stand out like a sore thumb. I was very easily embarrassed and that made me a target for teasing. I was glad when summer came and school was out.

When school started again in the fall of 1954, I had to take a physical education class. I have never liked any kind of sports except for volleyball, which I enjoyed playing when I was in the seventh grade. When it came time to do some physical tests, I couldn't even do one push-up. It wasn't funny to me but it was to everyone else. We could get a passing grade in the physical education class as long as we dressed in our gym clothes. I never undressed in front of the other boys. I would wait until the others were dressed and had left the locker room, and then hurriedly change.

At the end of class one day the teacher asked me to stay behind. When the others had left, he told me "I know you did it." When I asked him what he was talking about, he mentioned a boy by name and said "You stole his money!"

When I told him I hadn't stolen anything, he insisted, "I know you did."

I hadn't stolen anything and I was scared to death. I had never been in that kind of situation before (or since) and I had no idea what would happen to me. I was afraid he would contact my parents or even the police. He never said anything more about it. But, I never again felt comfortable around him. That was difficult for me because he was my homeroom teacher.

TWO

During the summer of 1955 while I was visiting a neighbor, she gave me a magazine that had an article about someone who had a sex-change operation. When she showed it to me, she asked me why I didn't have the operation. The idea excited me, but I was embarrassed that she connected me with the article. I had always wanted to be a girl and, in a way, I felt that I already was one inside. I had seen a newspaper article about the surgery, and I was already longing for it. Once I'd seen this second article, the surgery became my one and only goal.

As far as I was concerned, no other dream could come true until that goal had been realized. I was fifteen years old when school resumed in September, and I now knew my purpose in life. I was in the tenth grade, and I had military training as one of my classes. I found this class to be a nightmare. We had rifles that had to be cleaned and inspected weekly, and I always got demerits because I couldn't take my gun apart.

One day, we were marching on the field when one of the instructors had us halt. In front of the whole group, he imitated my walk. I was already self-conscious and could hardly keep from crying. By the next

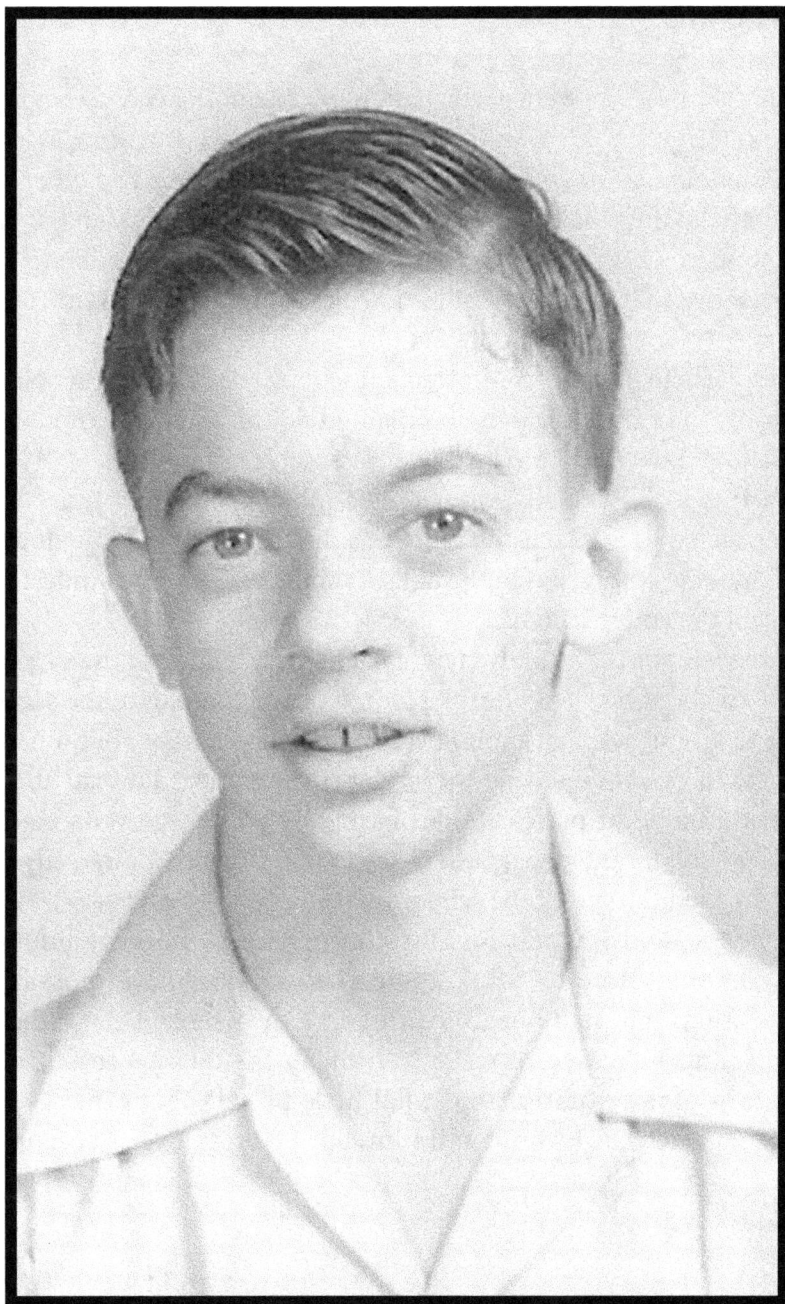

Tenth Grade

day, all my other classmates knew what had happened. Whether they knew me or not, they found it funny.

Another time, we were participating in a Memorial Day ceremony in Oakland Cemetery. It was extremely hot and we were standing at attention. Before I knew it, I was on the ground. I had fainted; two other boys also fainted. After that happened the others were told to stand at ease. At least no one laughed about that. The only time I liked military class was when we marched in parades down Peachtree Street in downtown Atlanta.

Despite being very uncomfortable at school, I did have a few friends—but never a best friend with whom I could do things. Throughout all of high school, I never once visited in a classmate's home.

I had two classes with a boy named John. At different times I had been attracted to boys but this time was different. I found myself going out of my way to pass him in the halls. I thought he was the kindest, cutest boy in the entire school.

By now, I was thoroughly convinced that I should have the surgery. I fantasized about how wonderful it would be if I could have the surgery, return to school, and have John become interested in me. But, I had no idea how to go about getting the surgery. The articles I'd read about it didn't talk about the practical side of arranging the surgery. As much as I hated school, I wanted to go just to see John. I think that's the only time I ever dreaded the end of the school year.

When school was out for the summer, I had nothing but time on my hands—time to think about, and realize the impossibility of, my situation. I had been listening to a minister on the radio for months, and I decided to write to him. In the letter, I told him all the details of my situation and what little I knew about the surgery. I also told him that I would call him, but I couldn't summon up the nerve.

COMPANY C

Commanded By CADET CAPTAIN JACK ANDERSON

High School Military Photo (third from right – back row)

Late that summer, I did some work for the company for which my father worked. I'm sure they let me work there as a favor to him. There wasn't much work for me to do and the job didn't pay much—only fifteen dollars a week before taxes. But, it did give me a little spending money and occupied my mind for a few hours each day.

One day during this time, I finally telephoned the minister I had written. I was so scared, I was dripping with perspiration. He told me that he knew nothing about the operation I wanted. He also assured me that, under the circumstances I had described to him, he could see nothing morally wrong or sinful about my wanting this surgery. This was something I desperately needed to hear. He didn't refer me to anyone or offer to counsel me, and he didn't have the solution to my problem. He was the first person to ever hear me say that I wanted to have sex-change surgery.

When school started again, it was worse than before. I was in my second year of military, with all the harassment that went with it; and there was John, who was also in military. I had missed seeing him during the summer, and seeing him was the only bright spot for me at school. Other girls also found him attractive. I was jealous, but I was certainly in no position to compete.

When it reached the point that seeing him caused too much pain, I did a complete turnabout and went out of my way to avoid him. I became very depressed, seeing no way that I could ever be happy. The whole situation became more than I could handle, and on September 16th, 1956, I was taken, unconscious to Grady Hospital. I had taken a handful of my mother's pain pills.

About the only thing I remember about the suicide attempt is my mother screaming when she found me. I could hear her but I couldn't say anything. After I had been in the emergency room for a while, I raised my head a little and tried to tell the attendant why I'd taken the pills. This sticks in my memory because I vividly remember him saying in a booming voice, "WHAAAT? LAY DOWN!" I never played with death again, but there would be many times in the years to come that I wished my suicide attempt had been successful.

It was several days before I could return to school. My nerves were shot, and I could hardly talk without crying. My parents made me go to a doctor. Before I went for my appointment, my father talked with the doctor. I felt as much at ease with him as with anyone else outside my family. He was elderly and had a grandfatherly demeanor.

As much as I wanted to tell him what was wrong, I couldn't seem to get out the words. Before going to him, I had written a letter to him describing my situation. Once I was in his office, I didn't have the nerve to give him the letter, much less tell him what was going on with me. I did make him understand how nervous I'd been. And, I asked him if he could get me out of military class, which he did.

Later, I mailed him the letter I'd written. In the letter, I wrote, "If you can't help me, I beg of you not to tell my father about the contents of this letter. I will kill myself if you do!"

The doctor never told my father what I'd written in the letter. I did learn that he told my father I was the most nervous person my age that he had ever seen. The doctor also gave my father the name of a psychiatrist and urged him to make an appointment for me to see him.

My parents did not mention the doctor's conversation with my father to me, thank God. Had my parents confronted me at that point in time, I would have made sure I succeeded where I had failed before. To bring my situation out into the open, with no solution in sight, would have destroyed any chance of normalcy that existed, be it pretense or otherwise. Without that, I could not have continued on.

I was halfway through eleventh grade; I couldn't endure another year and a half of school. My parents were very disappointed when I told them I wanted to quit school. The only reason I could give them was that I wanted to get a job. Mother was heartbroken and after several days of both of us crying, she finally consented, but I had to agree to go to a doctor. I quit school in November of 1956. Seventeen is a young age to start quitting. I think most people I came in contact with assumed I would never amount to anything. I didn't like quitting but there seemed to be nothing else I could do. I always hated having to say I quit school;

no one ever considered the possibility that there might have been a good reason for it.

It was a long time before I was mentally ready to look for a job. I was qualified for nothing and I looked twelve years old.

In those days when I envisioned myself as a female, it wasn't a thirty year old woman but a girl in her late teens. I envisioned myself as a teenage girl, having sex-change surgery and finishing high school. I wanted the high school experience as a girl.

In February of 1957, we moved from southeast Atlanta to Hapeville, a suburb of Atlanta. I was still at loss as to what to do, so I wrote to the psychiatrist recommended by the doctor I'd seen. I had found where my mother had hidden his name and I copied it for future use. I thought I might need it at some point. He responded, referring me to another doctor. I wrote to him and in his response he told me that such an operation was impossible.

Some months later I saw a newspaper article about Christine Jorgensen, who had the surgery. I sent the article to the doctor, again asking for his help. He referred me back to the psychiatrist. He also suggested that I move to another city and dress and live as a woman. This, to me was both impossible and undesirable as a solution. I was getting nowhere in any direction. I knew I had to do something, but I didn't know what it might be.

I decided to take a key punch course, thinking that I could use that skill later, after surgery. In the spring of 1957, I enrolled in a business school and completed the key punch course in August of that same year. I was the only male in the class. The school located a temporary part-time job for me shortly after I completed the course.

All the other operators were women, I felt ill at ease, but I relaxed after a few days. All my coworkers were friendly but I never formed a friendship with any of them. The less they knew about me, the better I liked it. There wasn't much I could have told them anyway.

I had a half-day work schedule and after work, I rushed home to watch American Bandstand and I listened to rock and roll on the radio at night. I didn't date, didn't know how to drive, and had no knowledge of—or interest in—the sorts of things men discussed. The job wasn't much but it occupied four hours of my day and gave me experience.

That September, I enrolled in evening high school. Surprisingly, I made very good grades. In October, I turned eighteen, and had to register for the draft. I was terrified of being drafted, and considered it the worst possible thing that could happen to me. I learned that it would be at least two years before I would be summoned for an examination. That was a big relief. I was sure I would have my problem solved before then.

I don't know how I thought I was going to bring that about because I sure didn't have a solution. If I didn't have it resolved, there was another way out, and I was sure I would take it if I had to. My previous experience had proved to me that at least death could be painless. True, I didn't die, but I went beyond the point of consciousness.

During this time, I saw another article concerning sex-change surgery. I was told many times afterwards that sex change surgery was out of the question. But, now, no matter how many times I heard it, I knew better.

In February of 1958, things started to go badly. I rode the bus to and from night school. One night after getting off the bus and crossing the street into my yard, I heard someone behind me. As I turned around, a man grabbed me and gruffly said, "Come here." I cried out, "You'd better leave me alone!" I jerked away from him and ran into the house.

My parents were already in bed, so I didn't tell them about it. I never returned to school because I was afraid the man would be watching for me. I never told my parents why I stopped going to school. During my parents' entire lives, I always shielded them from anything hurtful. I didn't want them worrying over how I was treated at school, work or anywhere else.

Within two weeks of that incident, my temporary job ended. I had hoped the job would become full-time, initially the supervisor had indicated that it probably would. I knew there hadn't been much work for me to do, but I was surprised when my supervisor told me that I was no longer needed.

During the next year and a half, I had some very bad times. I corresponded with several doctors, getting the same results as before. Many times I had difficulty convincing myself that any post-surgery life could be wonderful enough to make up for what I was going through then.

It was August of 1959 before I worked again. I got a job in the customer return department at Rich's, a large department store. I hated the job. My job was to replace merchandise damaged in Parcel Post and Railway Express. I interacted with many people in that position, including buyers and sales managers. I hated the job, but I hated life too, so why expect to like a job. My salary was forty dollars per week, and my take-home pay was thirty-two dollars. (By the time I left ten years later, I would be earning a grand eighty-four dollars per week and be the assistant manager of my department.)

The entire ten years that I worked at the store, I kept thinking I would be there just a few months longer. That's all that kept me going—believing, hoping, and praying that it would soon be over. One thing that was especially hard on me was the fact that there were several young men my age who worked in my department. That was the last thing I needed. Men that age can be the cruelest of all. I couldn't avoid them, but I couldn't be one of them either.

About two weeks after I started working there, I went to lunch with three of them. I sat by the only one I liked. I never knew what I did to make him ask me, "What are you; a queer? You keep on making passes!" I had no idea what I had done to make him say that, but it must have felt natural to me. I did the only thing I could to make sure I never repeated the mistake—I avoided him as much as possible.

The job entailed lifting heavy merchandise. In the beginning, it was very hard for me physically and I wanted to quit. But, I knew I couldn't keep quitting every time something went wrong. If I did, I would never get anywhere. Some of the boys delighted in embarrassing me. If they tried to bring me into their conversations, I would often pretend I hadn't heard what they'd said. They would laugh and say things like, "He don't like girls," or "I bet he ain't never had any," and other things just as embarrassing. Most of the boys were nice and I suppose all of them liked me.

The restroom was located one floor below my department. It was small and there was no privacy. If someone was in the restroom when I entered, I washed my hands and left. Then I would come back later.

Most of the boys didn't stay in the department very long. After a few years, I became the assistant supervisor, which meant a five-dollar-per week increase in salary and a lot more work. When the supervisor was out, I was responsible for an office staffed with five women and three to five young men. The women and I always got along fine. During the last few years I was there, I got along fine with most of the boys I supervised.

In 1960, I turned twenty-one, and still did not know which way to turn. My mother and an aunt used the same doctor. They were both impressed with him and considered him to be caring and understanding. So, I decided to write to him. I knew I was taking a chance, but I was desperate enough to risk it. With the letter I enclosed two post cards addressed to me. I put a different message on each card. One card, for example, was an invitation to join a bowling team.

I asked him to return one card if he could/would help me and the other if he couldn't. I received the card that indicated he couldn't help. One evening during mealtime, my mother mentioned that she'd seen the doctor. Then she said he'd questioned her about her children, especially me. She was quite puzzled, and I was on pins and needles until she dropped the subject.

1961 was a bad year—one of my worst. That summer I attended a family reunion. I didn't want to go, but my mother would have been disappointed if I had stayed home. Everything was fine until one of my aunts asked me where I worked. When I told her I worked in "the return department," she misunderstood me and thought I said the maternity department.

She said, "You would, you sissy thing!"

I was stunned, but she had no idea how much her remark hurt. It ruined the whole day for me. I vowed I would never attend another reunion.

I was in my twenty-second year and the draft board was becoming very interested in me. I was frequently receiving questionnaires. From the time I turned eighteen, I dreaded dealing with the draft board but I was sure I would get things worked out before things reached a critical point. Back then, I believed all I had to do was find the right doctor. I couldn't have been more wrong.

I decided it would be in my best interests to inform the draft board personnel of my situation. I wrote a letter telling them everything and giving them my work number. I don't know what I expected but it wasn't the call I received, instructing me to come in. My immediate reaction was panic.

It was several days before I could bring myself to call for an appointment. The lady I spoke with could not have been nicer. She assured me that everything was going to be fine. She did everything she could to make the ordeal as easy for me as possible. But, of course, she had rules she had to follow—inflexible rules. She arranged for me to see a private doctor for a physical examination. That examination provided no information to prevent them from sending me for a regular draft board physical.

The doctor I was sent to for the examination wasn't at all impressed with why I was there.

When the lady from the draft board called to tell me that I would have to go to the induction center for a regular physical, I told her I could not do that. She told me to try not to worry; she would see what she could do. She called a few days later to tell me that she had arranged for me to be examined alone before any of the others were called into the examination room. She assured me that she would be there on the day of the examination. I was afraid she would forget or something would go wrong. But, on that day, it happened just as she said it would.

There must have been between two and three hundred men in the gym-like waiting room. The first thing after roll call, I was called out into the hall. The lady from the draft board was waiting there to reassure me. My physical was completed before any of the others entered the examining room. There was a brief interview with a psychiatrist. Then, I waited in a room by myself all morning while the other physicals were completed. After lunch, I joined the others for the written examination.

I was so thankful when the day was over. The lady from the draft board who had helped me so much throughout the ordeal stuck with me until it was over. In November of 1961, I received my Statement of Acceptability indicating that I was unacceptable. My classification was 4-F. I requested that the reason for my classification be withheld when the results of my examination were mailed. This request was granted. Whenever I was asked why I was classified 4-F, I always said it was because of my bad back—a result of the wreck I had been in several years earlier.

It is impossible to describe how glad I was to have the draft board behind me because it is impossible to describe how much I feared it.

STATEMENT OF ACCEPTABILITY 101

LAST NAME - FIRST NAME - MIDDLE NAME

Smith, Jr. James Cleveland

PRESENT HOME ADDRESS

3637 Union Ave , Hapeville, Ga

SELECTIVE SERVICE NUMBER

9 | 64 | 39 | 626

LOCAL BOARD ADDRESS

L. B. # 64 Fulton County, Atlanta, Ga

LOCAL BOARD NO. 64
FULTON COUNTY

THE QUALIFICATIONS OF THE ABOVE-NAMED REGISTRANT HAVE BEEN CONSIDERED IN ACCORDANCE WITH THE CURRENT REGU-
LATIONS GOVERNING ACCEPTANCE OF SELECTIVE SERVICE REGISTRANTS AND HE WAS THIS DATE:

☐ 1. FOUND FULLY ACCEPTABLE FOR INDUCTION INTO THE ARMED FORCES.

☒ 2. FOUND NOT ACCEPTABLE FOR INDUCTION UNDER CURRENT STANDARDS.

ATLANTA 8, N. E.

DATE

22 Nov 61

PLACE

AFES, ATLANTA, GA

TYPED OR STAMPED NAME AND GRADE OF
JOINT EXAMINING AND INDUCTION STATION

CHARLEMPER. HILL JR.
CAPTAIN, INF.
DEP. CO., FOR INDUCTION

SIGNATURE

Albert A. Lee

DD FORM 62
1 MAR 59

PREVIOUS EDITIONS OF THIS FORM ARE OBSOLETE.

REGISTRANT COPY 2

Any inquiry relative to personal status should be referred to your Local Board

Notification From Draft Board

20

My Brother Billy

THREE

In September of 1961, I began a two-year accounting course at the business school I had attended for the key punch course. I went to school at night and my father met my bus. I still had not learned to drive, and I was afraid to walk from the bus line to my home. My enrollment for this course was a big mistake and I didn't do very well. My old worries combined with having to deal with the draft board were about all my mind could handle.

In October, my brother left for the Marines, and my grandfather died the same day. In November of that year, my father was almost killed when he was hit by a fast moving train. I was at work when I received the news. I almost fainted and couldn't remember which hospital he was taken to. When I was composed enough, my supervisor drove me to the hospital we thought he would be taken to, but I'd gotten the name of the hospital wrong.

When we finally arrived at the correct hospital, I expected to find my father dead. He was badly injured. His back was covered with a huge bruise, he had cuts and broken bones, and his spleen was ruptured and had to be removed. He was in the hospital for a month. I had to quit my accounting course, but I didn't even care. In fact, it was a relief.

My brother was unable to come home during my father's hospitalization or recovery period. Most of his time in the Marines was spent in the hospital. He was diagnosed with chronic bronchitis and eventually received a medical discharge. He was very thin when he arrived home.

The next year was very hard. For the first part of the year, my father was basically an invalid. He had already been living with certain infirmities since the 1953 car wreck. He had only one eye from the childhood baseball incident, and his left arm was numb to the point where he couldn't even feel a bee sting. With these new injuries on top of the old ones, many people would have given up.

Daddy had been driving a cement mixer when he was hit by the train. When he stopped at the railroad crossing, he looked both ways for oncoming traffic. First, in the direction that the train was about to come around a curve—and in that moment, it was clear. He then looked in the opposite direction, which was also clear. Because the cement mixer was running, and noisy, my father never heard the train coming.

He received a little bit of settlement money from the train wreck, and used that money to buy a small dump truck. That way, he could work on his own terms, when he was able. At first, he wasn't able to work very much. By spring of the following year—1963—he was working most of the time, even though he often didn't feel up to it.

Once Daddy was doing better, I again turned my attention to my personal problem. I rented a mailbox and began writing to doctors in all fields. I also wrote to medical universities and to anyone (even politicians) I thought might be able to offer me any assistance or encouragement, or point me to someone who could. Some people didn't respond at all, and the replies I did receive were varied. Many referred me to someone else. Some were sympathetic, some were not. Some suggested I was crazy, while couching their message in pleasant words. One led me to believe he would help me just to find out all he could.

By the beginning of 1964, I was spending every moment that I was not asleep or at work writing letters. I wrote to a local columnist, a "Dear Abby" type who was very helpful. Though we never met, we talked several times by phone and she acted as a forwarding service for some of the letters I received from people I did not want to know my identity. I trusted no one with the news flash that I wanted to have sex-change surgery.

The following is the contents of a letter to me forwarded by the columnist.

"Dear Amy Larkin:

An unknown patient wrote to me on April first, enclosing a great deal of other material including copies of letters to a doctor. If a patient has not sufficient confidence in a doctor to give him his full name, he does not really deserve an answer or any kind of help. However, I have seen a great many patients with a very similar problem and know how much disturbed they are emotionally, and therefore, I will tell you what I think so that you can transmit the information to the patient. Also, please see to it that he reads the enclosed reprint.

Judging by all the correspondence, there seems very little doubt that this patient is a transsexual. Very few physicians in this country know anything about this condition and many don't want to know about it because they have been prejudiced by sensational 'sex change' operations reported in tabloid papers. But transsexuals are among the unhappiest people I have ever seen in my practice and do deserve help. Psychotherapy has proved completely useless as far as any cure is concerned.

In a case like this unknown patient's, I have found treatment with female hormone (estrogen) distinctly useful as it relieves them of a great deal of their emotional strain.

If you know of a doctor who is interested in this patient, ask him to write to me, giving me some more information about this patient (he didn't even tell me his age) and if possible, the result of a hormone assay in a 24 hour specimen of urine to determine the so-called 17 ketosteroids. I could then send this doctor one of my more technical reprints from a medical journal dealing with this subject.

These patients are only temporarily 'appeased' by estrogen treatment and would still want the operation. I am not a surgeon (nor am I a psychiatrist) and do not know of anyone in this country competent and willing to perform this kind of operation. There are places in Europe or Japan where it could be done but this would cost a great deal of money which this patient does not have.

Sincerely,

Harry Benjamin, MD"

As far as I was concerned, his letter and the reprint were documentation but he provided me with no solution. It is interesting to note that, in a letter received from this same doctor after I had the surgery, he stated: "IF YOU CAN TAKE A DOCTOR IN ATLANTA INTO YOUR CONFIDENCE AND LET HIM OBSERVE THE CHANGES, THAT MAY BE BEST..."

The columnist made an appointment for me to see an endocrinologist. This specialist was pleasant but had no knowledge in the area I that needed help, despite having seen the letter from Dr. Benjamin and read the reprint. He told me that what I wanted could not be done. I didn't go back to him, but every time I learned something new on the subject of transsexualism, I sent him a copy.

Almost every night, I worked on a letter to someone. In September of 1964, I wrote to Governor Carl Sanders of Georgia, who forwarded my letter to the Dean of the Medical College of Georgia. I received a letter from the Dean, informing me that the surgery was illegal in Georgia. I wrote to medical schools all over the country, two of which kept me dangling for several months. One of the medical schools finally informed me that they did not do that type of surgery at their school.

I corresponded with a plastic surgeon at one school for several months. He had me believing for a while that they would accept me as a teaching patient—a guinea pig. After a while he told me that I should go to Vocational Rehabilitation (VR) here in Georgia because "each state takes care of its own." I was very disappointed. I couldn't understand why it took him so long to tell me no. When this possibility fell through, I sank into a deep depression. My parents were very worried about me, and I could not explain anything to them.

In October, I contacted the Department of Family and Children Services. On October 13th, 1965, the following letter was sent to Mr. F. E. Wynn, supervisor of the District Vocational Rehabilitation Office.

"Dear Mr. Wynn:

Enclosed is a 'confidential' letter which I would like to refer to you for your consideration. Even though this party indicates that he is working, it is not stated in what capacity or whether continuously. Inasmuch as this seems to involve a combination of psychological issues, possible surgery and restoration, and/or training or retraining for some vocation, you may wish to assign the case for exploration to one of your counselors.

Yours very truly,

Wellborn R. Ellis, Administrator,

Fulton County Dept. of Family and Children Services"

I was twenty-six years old and already thinking that what should have been the best years of my life were now over. I felt like, even if I was able to arrange the surgery, I was getting too old for any kind of life post-surgery. But, if I was going to live, I had to do so with all determined efforts.

Shortly after I received a copy of the above letter, I had my first appointment with a VR counselor. Imagine my delight when he told me that the surgery could be done here in Georgia at the medical college! I completely disregarded the previous information I'd received, and believed him. I thought to myself, *Why would he lie?*

First, the VR counselor said that I would need to see a physician who would recommend that I be evaluated by an endocrinologist. I was allowed to select the physician that I preferred to see. I chose the doctor I had been sent to by the draft board because he was familiar with my case. He was no more delighted to see me this time than he was the first time, but my spirits were so high, I couldn't care less what he thought. He gave me the needed recommendation.

With this doctor's recommendation, the VR counselor told me that he would make an appointment with the endocrinologist who worked in conjunction with the surgeon at the medical college. He seemed to think there would be no problems.

Just prior to my contact with VR, I had corresponded with a reporter who had written some articles that interested me. He became interested in my situation and wanted to do an article about me. Even though my name wouldn't be used in the article, I was a little afraid that it might jeopardize VR's willingness to help me. The VR counselor assured me that it would not. The article follows.

LONG-ILL TIM GETS NEW HOPE TO SOLVE ENDOCRINE MALADY

In his own words, Tim is one of nature's "freaks".

He feels he is "a prisoner", like a woman in a man's body. He is not a criminal, nor a pervert. He has not harmed society. If anything society has harmed him.

He is a slender, shy man with a medical problem few others in the country have. Doctors know little about it and seem reluctant to become involved.

For a very few there has been relief in "sex-change" operations – almost always in foreign countries. The operations are costly and Tim has little money. He also has invalid parents to care for.

Tim tried to find help for years. He wrote doctors, psychiatrists, medical centers, political figures, ministers, other "sex-change" patients, even advice columnists.

For years Tim has been referred from one to the next. He has been told to dress and live as a woman. He has been told he may have a hormone imbalance. He has been warned that the operations are complicated, painful and inconclusive, that they require far-reaching adjustments.

Tim isn't a doctor. He knows only what he feels – and that he needs help.

At times help has seemed near, but always elusive. It seems near again. A State agency has said he might qualify for expense-paid treatment in Augusta (GA). Decisions are pending.

Recently, when his hopes were at their lowest, Tim wrote The Atlanta Constitution and told his story in lengthy letters and essays. Names have been changed to protect identities, but this is his story collected from the things he wrote.

Nature made a freak of me. My appearance is that of a male, a very feminine male. I have hair on my chest, arms and legs and I shave every day.

My thoughts, my desires, everything I ever wanted had only one requirement and that was to be a female. I am sure I was born this way. When I was a small child, it was evident that I was not normal. I preferred dolls rather than cowboy guns. I always played with girls and was accepted as one of them.

I even cried for my mother to buy me little girl dresses. I loved playing 'playhouse' with girls. I didn't get along well with boys. They were always picking on me.

Being called a sissy was not new to me when I started to school. By the time I was in the fourth grade, I was very shy. I tried to act like a boy but I failed in every way. I tried playing softball at school and my classmates would say "you hold the bat just like a girl".

There were many embarrassing situations during my grade school years. I was always glad for school to be out for the summer. I thought, next year they won't remember to call me sissy, but they did.

The first time I was called a queer I was in the ninth grade. I didn't know what a queer was.

Always wishing I had been a girl, it seemed natural that any romantic inclinations I had would be toward the male sex. It didn't alarm me. I liked the feeling.

Soon after entering the eleventh grade, I almost had a nervous breakdown. I didn't want to live as I was. I took a handful of pills and was carried to the hospital unconscious.

The incident left me so nervous that I couldn't stand to be in school. I could hardly keep from screaming sometimes. When I was home, I cried a lot, especially at night when I was in bed. I pleaded with my parents to let me quit school. They finally gave in. They said I could quit only if I agreed to go to a doctor. I could give them no reasons for anything.

There followed the years of visits and letters. Tim kept his problem from his parents. He led a quiet stay-at-home life. Now he is in his mid-twenties.

I don't go to church or anywhere else (except work) because of this problem. I don't and cannot act as a male is supposed to. I don' t talk man talk. In fact, it embarrasses me. I never have anything to add to the conversation and it is soon noticed. It has been suggested that I take courses that would enable me to get a better job, but I am so nervous and afraid that I can't talk freely with relatives, much less enroll in a class which would put me with young adults who would expect me to be one of them.

I have not done anything to be ashamed of. I have never been involved in any kind of homosexual activities and I am not ashamed of myself.

I do not feel that my mind is abnormal in any way. I feel the abnormality is my body only. This affliction does not make me less human than anyone else.

Dick Hebert

The Atlanta Constitution

After several days passed and I had not heard from my VR counselor, I called him. I was told that he was no longer there, and another counselor would return my call. I had to make several attempts before another counselor finally spoke with me. The new counselor said that he would make the appointment for me to see the endocrinologist. The appointment was made and I saw the doctor the following week.

It was terrible. He was very rude. He said that he saw a certain number of patients for VR each month, and felt that I was taking up time that could be better spent on someone who really needed it. He seemed to think it was his duty to stop me from wasting so many people's time. I felt that I was repulsive to him, and I was not prepared for his attitude.

He examined me but was totally uninterested in why I was there. I was scared and nervous when I went in for the appointment but that was a good feeling compared to how I felt afterwards. I thought I would be coming back, perhaps several times if he worked in conjunction with the surgeon. He discussed nothing about any procedures or treatments, and I never saw him again.

A few days later, I called my new VR counselor, Larry Walker, to see if he had heard from the doctor. He said he had not, but I doubted that he was telling the truth. He said he wanted me to come in so that he could meet me and get to know me. When we met, he seemed nice enough, and made it clear that he knew nothing about sex-change surgery. He asked me so many questions and with every answer I gave him, he asked, "Why?"

By the time I left, he knew just about everything I knew on the subject, which really wasn't much. I left there believing he understood that I *had* to go through with surgery and there was no changing my mind. A few days later, my VR counselor let me know he'd heard from the doctor, and asked me to come back in.

This time he was a totally different person. He was now an expert on the subject of transsexualism, telling me what could and could not be done. He seemed delighted to tell me that the doctor did not recommend the surgery. He further told me that he had talked with a psychiatrist who had told him that he didn't think treatment would help me.

The VR counselor went on to say that he'd talked with someone at the Georgia Mental Health Institute, and that they would be interested in working with me. He said I would have to go to the Mental Health Institute on my own, without a referral from VR. He said there was nothing else that VR could or would do until I went to the institute.

It was clear to me that something had gone horribly wrong. The first VR counselor seemed quite knowledgeable about sex-change surgery. He even mentioned the doctor's name that would do the surgery here in Georgia. I tried to locate the original VR counselor but no one in VR would give me any information. No matter what the second counselor had told me, I couldn't dismiss what the first counselor had told me. Anyway, I knew the second counselor was lying. I was convinced that VR wasn't doing their job.

I decided to write a letter to the endocrinologist that VR had sent me to. I told him that I didn't know what he had told my VR counselor, but whatever he had said was unacceptable to me. I also said that he had barely acknowledged why I was being sent to him because he was too busy telling me off. He replied that VR did not request a recommendation from him, and he had offered none, except to recommend that I be referred to a psychiatrist.

I sent a copy of his letter to the VR counselor. A keg of dynamite would have achieved the same reaction. He called and asked me to come into his office the next day. I went but I immediately regretted it. It had never occurred to him that I would contact the doctor on my own. Apparently, he thought he could dismiss me and that would be the end of that. He was furious at me for going behind his back. For the first few minutes, he said nothing. He just sat and stared at me.

Then, he began to ask me questions about my relationship with my parents, wanting to know what kinds of things we discussed. I told him I talked with them about everything except my problem. He told me he did not believe that. Then he asked me about my relationship with my coworkers, and implied I had discussed my situation with them. I told him again that I had not discussed my problem with anyone.

He was getting more and more angry. He brought up all the letters I'd written to people, seeking help and telling them about what I wanted to do. He said that I'd written all the letters because I *enjoyed* my situation. Finally, he asked me what I thought about him and I declined to comment. I hated his guts—but I don't think I hated him as much as he hated me.

In hindsight, I think of him as temperamental, unprofessional, unfit and unqualified for his profession. He was the rudest grownup I'd ever encountered at that point in my life. I also think his inability to handle my case made him look like a fool in the eyes of his peers.

I had to be careful not to say or do anything that would make him feel warranted in closing my case. I asked him what he would do if the Mental Health Institute recommended the surgery. He said, "We will cross that bridge when we come to it." I didn't know it then, but he knew all along that they wouldn't. I doubt that he ever even spoke with them. I certainly never saw any proof that he had.

I was so upset when I left his office, I had to walk a few blocks in order to compose myself enough to board a bus. It was all I could do to keep from crying. I went to bed early and cried, praying that I would die. I saw no way I could ever be happy, and felt that nothing could be worth the hell I was going through.

I was on the verge of a nervous breakdown. I was constantly being asked what was wrong. Someone even commented that I looked like a zombie.

My parents became even more concerned about me. I hurt their feelings almost every day by telling them to "just leave me alone." I knew my family loved me, and it would have broken their hearts if they had known what I was going through. I saw no reason for them to suffer when there was nothing they could do to help me

FOUR

My thoughts again turned to suicide. The only thing that kept me alive was my desire to not hurt my parents. Sometimes I overruled that "noble" reason for wanting to live, reasoning that continuing to live as I was living would eventually cause them more heartache than my death. I was certain I would lose my mind if I didn't get help—and my hope that help was coming had evaporated. At times, I thought it would be a blessing if I did lose my mind. At least insanity would be an escape from a life I found unbearable.

It was days before I could even want to try again. The first thing I did was to advise the reporter what had happened. The following is his reply.

Dear J. C.,

I've read with interest your letter and copy of the letter to Mr. Walker. I confess, I don't know what I can do for you or even what action you yourself should take. I feel any interference by me personally would only jeopardize your case with the state and medical profession. There seems one avenue left to you, from your letters—that of going to the Mental Health Institute. I can't say whether they would be of any help or not; I would definitely advise keeping in touch with Mr. Walker, also, because he has not necessarily closed the door on your case.

As you can see, I only have a few scattered thoughts left on this case. I do want to know how it progresses. In any event, it does not seem likely that anyone will allow you to undergo the operation until you have exhausted all other means, including psychiatric. This is why I advise going to the institute. Perhaps, one day our medical geniuses will be enlightened enough to treat humanity for what ails it, without prejudice and small-mindedness. Until then, we just have to keep plugging along. You have done the job admirably, and I hope you don't give up the struggle. You have to make do with what is available, and it is likely that the best help available at present is psychiatry. I do not know. I can only guess. I wish you luck and let me hear from you.

Your friend

Dick Hebert

I decided to take the advice of Mr. Hebert. On January 25, 1966, I wrote the following letter to the Mental Health Institute.

Dear Sir;

The enclosed material describes my problem and how I wish to solve it. In reading this material, you will learn of my progress and handicaps. Mr. Larry Walker at the Vocational Rehabilitation Department said he talked with someone at the Mental Health Institute and was told the

Institute would be interested in working with me. I understand there will be no charge for this.

As far as any cure is concerned, you cannot help me via treatment or otherwise. What do I expect from this consultation? A recommendation from you that I have the surgery. I would like the recommendation as soon as possible. After I have the surgery, I would like to continue having sessions with you. That is when I can benefit from it.

The problem at hand is that I am scared to come to you. I am afraid, nervous, and embarrassed, but not ashamed. If any papers have to be filled out, could you mail them to me and let me return them to you or bring them with me? When I come to you (even the first time) I want someone to be expecting me; maybe an appointment could be set up. Mr. Walker led me to believe I just needed to show up.

I am enclosing a reprint written by a doctor (Dr. Harry Benjamin) who probably knows more about transsexuals than anyone else. It supports my description of myself 100 per cent. May I hear from you soon?

Sincerely,

J. C. Smith

P.S. Mr. Walker (VR counselor), told me you would rather I come on my own rather than be recommended by him. I cannot force myself to come unannounced and tell why I am there.

In response to my letter, The Mental Health Institute sent me an application for voluntary admission, which I returned to them on February 15th, 1966. In the application, I had to make a statement of my problem and my reason for applying for treatment. The statement I submitted was as follows:

> *I want to change my sex. I feel that I am mentally female, physically male. All my life I have wanted to be a female. I know of no condition or incident that could provoke this problem. I feel that I was born with this affliction, and to have my physical sex changed via surgery is the only answer. I could live and function as a woman. By function, I mean I could do what I want to do. I could live as a normal woman except that I could not have children.*

> *I did not make this decision without any thought. Ever since I learned this surgery could be done, I have thought of nothing else. I have never made any plans as to what I would do when I became a man, but many plans as to what I would do when I became a woman. I am 26 years old. If I don't have this surgery soon, it will be too late to have thoughts of any kind of career.*

> *In 1961, I started an accounting course at a business school. I dropped out when my father was injured in a train wreck. I kept waiting for a better time to go back. I cannot get my mind off wanting to change my sex. I could not learn anything with this on my mind all the time. Time has become very important. What should have been the best years of my life are now over. No one has the right to make this decision for me. I am not crazy. I know what I would be doing. It [having sex-change surgery] would be difficult; it is more difficult now [to live without the surgery]. As I*

am now, there is no place for me. I only want to be myself without fear. I want others to know me as I am.

My sole purpose for coming to you at this point is the hope that you will recommend to VR that I should have this surgery, the sooner the better. After the surgery, you could, I am sure, help me to make a more complete adjustment. There is no changing my mind about the surgery. Treatment cannot make me want to be a male. There is no other answer to my problem but the surgery.

If there is no prejudice, you will agree. I don't think it should take you long to come to this conclusion after reading this and other data and asking questions that have arisen from reading such. Your conclusion can only be your opinion, not factual. You could not prove any point to me, nor could I to you, but the object is for me to be happy, if that is possible. I am very scared to come to you.

This is too difficult for me, and no one I have turned to has tried to make it easier for me. I know it will be difficult for me to talk to you; I will be so nervous, I can't think clearly. I am and will be completely honest with you, and it is my hope that I will get a strong recommendation that I have this surgery as soon as possible.

Sincerely,

J. C. Smith

I was put on a waiting list and apparently forgotten. On May 30th, I wrote the following letter:

More than eight weeks have passed since your letter advising me that it would be no longer than eight weeks that I would have to wait for the evaluation. Can you tell me when to expect to hear from you? I was instructed to "not write again" and that they would contact me as soon as possible.

On July 29th, I wrote again.

Dear Sir,

In your letter to me dated February 25, 1966, you stated that I had been placed on a waiting list. I wrote to you and asked how long it would be before my time would come. You answered via letter March 21, "it may be six to eight weeks before your evaluation; however, it may be a shorter time than that. I do not expect it to go beyond eight weeks."

It has been more than five months since February 25th. I wrote you again in June and was advised "it is necessary to put your name on a waiting list."

When I saw my first VR counselor on the first of December last year, he talked as if the whole thing would be over in a few weeks, surgery included. I worried that it was happening too fast all of a sudden. Obviously, I need not have worried about that. I feel that I am further away from the surgery now than I was then.

Doctor, I know you are as tired of my letters as I am of writing them. If I am not going to be contacted for this evaluation, please tell me. I cannot believe the waiting list has prohibited me from being contacted before now. There must be another reason. Perhaps it is hoped that I will give up—I won't.

Finally, in the latter part of August of 1966, I was summoned to the Mental Health Institute for consultation. I was ushered into a room where I found seventeen people seated at a table. Some appeared friendly (actually two people); most appeared to be disgusted. I was overwhelmed. I had been dreading seeing even *one* person. They put me through the mill that day. I survived by directing my attention to just two of the men, who seemed more interested in helping me than any of the others.

I never did relax, and when I left, I hardly remembered anything about the ordeal. I went back three or four more times for written evaluations and more interviews, etc. In the end, they concluded that I was "capable of making up my own mind." I thought their decision that I was capable of making up my own mind would mean that VR would proceed in the direction of the surgery I was seeking. It meant that no further action was required from the mental health institute.

At the time, I was encouraged by their decision, and immediately contacted VR. This time I was assigned yet another counselor, and had to start all over again. At least the new counselor treated me like a human being. After a while, he sent me to another psychiatrist, who seemed determined to change my mind about the surgery. He did some weird things, but I was naïve and accepted his explanations of his strange behavior. After all, he was the doctor and I was supposedly the sick one.

For example, when he tried to kiss me, he said he wanted to see what I would do. Another time, he tried to burn me with a cigarette. He said he wanted to see if I would defend myself. (It was only after my surgery that things became clear. That's when another of his patients, referred to me by an organization interested in the welfare of transsexuals, related his experience to me. This patient shared with me the fact that the doctor had taken photos of him in the nude. At that point, I put all the pieces together, and concluded that this doctor had problems of his own. He certainly was not the doctor I needed to see. Yet, he had been allowed—and paid—to make very important decisions about my life and there was nothing I could do about it. Needless to say, VR was negligent in sending patients to such a doctor.)

The last time I saw this particular doctor, he told me I was the most stubborn person he had ever seen. At least he was right about one thing. But, in the end he also agreed that I was capable of making up my own mind about the surgery.

I outlasted Vocational Rehabilitation. The counselor finally told me that VR couldn't help me because I was employed. They had known this from the very beginning, even before they saw me the first time. During my first interview, I had been told that my salary was not sufficient to disqualify me for their services. During my final appointment with my last VR counselor, I was told that the second counselor (Mr. Walker) was overheard telling someone that he was putting my file in the bottom of a drawer and hoped he never heard of me again.

VR apparently never intended to help me. Yet they had no choice but to deal with my request for help, especially since I had been referred to them by another state agency. I suppose they expected to wear me out so I would give up. I was at my wit's end and I had only two choices—keep trying or end it all. The only way I can explain my ability to keep going is to attribute it to God's will. Otherwise, I don't know how—or why—I could have gone on.

I wanted the governor of Georgia to know about my experience with VR and wrote him a letter. In his reply of November 13th, he stated:

> *"There is no possible way that any of the agencies of State Government can assist you financially or otherwise. I am sorry that I have offered so little encouragement to you but I do hope that you understand that I am sympathetic to your situation. My prayer is that you will continue to seek guidance from Above in your search for happiness in the future."*

Sincerely,

Lester Maddox

Governor of Georgia

(He would still be governor when I began working for the state in November of 1970. Near Christmas, he visited the state offices, wearing a Santa Claus suit. He hugged all the girls, including me, and wished us a Merry Christmas.)

FIVE

———

Throughout the sixties, I rode the bus to and from work. Around 1967, two girls who may have been thirteen or fourteen years old rode the same bus I did. For some reason they zeroed in on me. They stood beside me until they could sit next to me and loudly teased me and laughed. One of them asked my name and told me her name was Pussy Galore. My embarrassment was hilarious to them. I did not recognize the name as that of the character from the 1964 movie *Goldfinger*. I tried catching a later bus. The next day they changed buses too. They continued to harass me until school was out for the summer.

One day at work in late 1968, I was asked by a coworker/friend and a friend of his that I casually knew to go out to eat. Afterwards we stopped by the apartment of a friend of theirs. While we were there their friend and his roommate started kissing. I will never forget how shocked I was; I had never seen men kissing. It had not occurred to me that my friends were gay. (They visited me after my surgery in 1969 and told me that they thought I was gay and planned to bring me out into the open.)

On February 6th, 1968, the late Dr. Walter Alvarez answered a letter I had written him:

"I sympathize deeply. I finally found a surgeon here in Chicago who is very able and willing to perform the operation; the difficulty is to find a hospital in which the work can be done...."

At last, I had the name of a surgeon who was willing and able to perform the operation! There was only one catch: the doctor's fee was $8,500.00. It might as well have been a million. I didn't have the money and had no way to get it.

One day not long after I received the encouraging letter from Dr. Alvarez, I saw Christine Jorgensen on Merv Griffin's television show. I wrote to Mr. Griffin, asking if he could give me an address for her. Within two weeks, I received a card from him, giving me Christine Jorgensen's address. I immediately wrote, and soon received a letter from her, giving me the name of a doctor who could put me in touch with a surgeon.

I soon had a reply from the doctor, giving me the names and addresses of two surgeons who did the surgery for $3,000.00. One was in Tijuana, Mexico and the other in Casablanca, Morocco. I wrote to both of them, using a translation service to write my letter in French to the doctor in Casablanca and then translate the reply. By the time I received the reply from the doctor in Casablanca and had it translated, I had decided to use the doctor in Mexico.

I had no idea what I was going to do, or how. I only knew that I would find a way, no matter what. I considered every avenue I could think of, and finally came up with a plan. It was going to be very difficult. In September of 1968, I wrote to Dr. Jesus Barbosa, the doctor in Mexico. In my letter, I asked him to make arrangements for the surgery to take place in early 1969, and requested that he advise me as soon as possible of the date.

When he replied, he advised me that his fee had gone up to $4,000.00. That was still less than half the fee charged by the surgeon mentioned by Dr. Alvarez.

I was ready to put my plan into action—but first, I had to confide in one person. I told that person the whole story and asked if I could stay in his home until I left for the surgery. When he recovered from the shock of what I had told him, he told me I could stay as long as I needed to. He also said he would help me in any way that he could.

My parents just couldn't understand why I moved out. It was certainly out of character for me. I rarely went anywhere. They would know the truth all too soon. I knew they would be greatly concerned by this move and I dreaded that day for them.

January 17th, 1969 was the last day on my job. I had given my supervisor a two-week notice and requested he tell no one. The ladies with whom I worked were older and mothered me, and I knew they would be concerned. They were completely baffled because I was leaving and would tell them nothing. I instructed them not to call my parents under any circumstances.

(A couple of years later, my supervisor told me he knew I wanted to have the surgery, although he would not reveal how he knew. I had corresponded with an official at Rich's to inquire if my insurance might pay anything toward the surgery, but I did not sign my name. I used as my return address my P.O. box at the post office located across the street from Rich's. Obviously, the store official had my post office box watched to see who picked up my mail.

On my last day of work, I sent a Special Delivery letter to my supervisor rescinding my resignation. I fully expected to return to my job after the surgery, and had resigned only to allow the supervisor to arrange for my desk to be covered while I was away.

On Sunday, January 19th, 1969, I called my brother's wife and asked her to meet me at the place where I was staying. When she arrived, I didn't invite her in. I stepped outside and told her I was about to leave for the airport. I was dressed in traveling clothes, and had a suitcase at the door to make my story convincing. I gave her an envelope to take to my brother, and asked her to tell him to take the letter to my parents. I told her the letter was urgent and that they must receive the letter that day.

The letter read as follows:

January 18, 1969

Dear Mother and Daddy,

Maybe I have handled this wrong. I don't know. I hope you will understand. I am happier than I have ever been, or at least I will be after this is all behind me. There is no need for you to be unhappy for me.

Read the enclosed reprint (describing sex-change surgery). I need $4,200.00 for this surgery. I am sure you can borrow that much on the house. I will pay it back. Send it to my post office address here in town. My doctor will forward it to me in Los Angeles. You will not have to explain this to anyone. I will write a letter to everyone that matters. I need this money before the 28th of January which is only ten days away. Jack [minister/uncle] knows about this. Send my birth certificate also. I have to have it.

I will write in a few days. Do not be hurt or upset by this. I'm not.

Love,

J. C.

There was no doctor picking up my mail. I had it picked up by the man with whom I was staying. I didn't want my parents to know I was still in town because I couldn't bear to see them before my surgery.

My parents knew nothing of my intentions before receiving this letter. No one could have handled it better than they did. I had told them in the letter that I would be in California, but I didn't actually go until I received the money. The waiting time was nerve-racking, and I hardly left the house. While I was waiting, I sent the following letter to all the people who would need to know.

Dear _____;

This letter will surprise you but, knowing me as you do, you will realize how true it is and has been. Nature made a freak of me. I am not bitter. I am just so glad that I can now be my true self. I am not the male I was brought up to be. I am female. I am not the only one this has happened to, nor will I be the last.

Needless to say, life for me has been almost unbearable much of the time. I tried to pretend it didn't matter, but it hurt so very much. Almost everyone I know has hurt me in this way because of the situation; some not realizing it, others thoroughly enjoying it. I had to quit school because of this situation, not because of something I had done or been involved in. I was about to have a nervous breakdown. I have been almost a recluse for the past ten years, hardly ever going anywhere but to work. Not because I didn't want to but because I knew if I did go anywhere there would be unpleasantness when my secret became known.

I am sending a great many people a copy of this letter. I hope you all can and will accept me. I do not beg you to; some of you will accept me; others can't and won't. I do not want anyone to think they will be doing me a favor to be seen with me. If you can't accept me, tell me now. I will understand. I will not push myself on anyone. If I will have caused anyone any embarrassment, I am sorry. I will be heavily in debt for several years. I cannot worry about who likes me and who doesn't.

I will not live in the past and I will not discuss my past life with you now or ever. There is no need for it. Do not question my parents because they know little more than you. I am not really a freak, but a victim of unfortunate circumstances. I certainly did not ask to have this problem. Be thankful it didn't happen to you.

J. C.

When I received the money from my parents, I picked up my plane ticket and got a four-thousand-dollar cashier's check. Along with the money, I received a letter from my parents in which they assured me of their love and told me not to worry, we would all start over somewhere else.

Finally everything was all set. I was tired of hiding out, and relieved to be leaving Atlanta. I had planned to leave on January 29th but heavy fog prevented any planes from departing that day. I finally did get out the next day. Shortly after I was seated, a middle-aged man and his wife sat next to me. After introductions and brief conversation, I discovered that he was a doctor with whom I had corresponded in 1960! Just my luck.

I decided to ignore them, but he was persistent. He was reading a book on civilizations of the world. Several times, he asked me to read a paragraph and tell him what I thought about it. He asked me a lot of questions about why I was going to California and what I did back in Atlanta. I was afraid he was going to remember my correspondence with him. He had been my mother's doctor for several years. (I wrote him a note while I was recovering from my first operation. Afterwards, he always asked my aunt, who was also his patient, about me. I saw him again in 1974. He was very nice and seemed genuinely happy to see me.)

SIX

By the time I arrived in Los Angeles, I was exhausted. I discovered that I could not get a direct flight into Tijuana. According to the airlines, I could fly into Mexico City or San Diego. In either case, the next flight was several hours away. I checked the train and bus schedules and found that there would be a few hours wait, regardless of the mode of transportation. I decided on the train. It was about a three-hour-ride to San Diego.

I arrived around one o'clock Friday morning. Once there, I learned that the border was just a few miles away. I would have to take a taxi or bus to the border. Taxi fares were eating away my funds. Along the way, someone told me I couldn't cross the border in a public vehicle. I arrived at the border just before 2 a.m.

The guard at the border pointed towards a dark area ahead and said, "There are taxis over there." I was filled with anxiety, but there was no turning back. I walked for what felt like a half mile or so before I reached the taxis, and I was no less scared when I found them. As I walked to the taxis, I prayed to God, that if it was wrong for me to have this surgery, don't let it happen. The drivers looked like hoodlums to me. The drivers of several different taxis opened their car doors for me, I chose a driver who spoke English. He was very kind—a friend indeed.

I had been told that the Americana Hotel was a nice place to stay, but the hotel was no longer in existence. The driver told me that the Caesar Hotel was the nicest hotel in Tijuana, and it probably had been—in 1925. I had to walk upstairs to reach my room, as there was no elevator. The curtains were at least a foot shorter than the windows but, as bad as it was, my room looked good to me. I was so tired.

I went to bed immediately. I had covered a lot of ground, even considering it had been a twenty-eight-hour period. It was very noisy outside the hotel, but I slept soundly, waking only once to the sound of someone vomiting in the next room.

It was mid-morning when I awoke again. I had a bath, called my doctor's office, and advised the nurse that I would be there about one o'clock in the afternoon. When I went down to have breakfast, I somehow overlooked the hotel restaurant.

I went outside onto the street, looking for some place to eat. What I saw was unbelievable—a whole different world. I saw a lady with a homemade, portable hot dog stand. It looked very untidy and I couldn't stomach the idea. There was no restaurant in sight, and I wasn't about to go exploring. As I stood there, trying to figure out what to do, a man approached me and asked if I wanted a woman. I hurried back into the hotel, and once inside, I spotted the restaurant. I knew I should eat because I had no idea what to expect when I left the hotel.

When I did leave, I checked out, fully expecting to enter the hospital later in the day. The doctor's office was on the second floor of one of the very few modern buildings that I saw in Tijuana. Once I arrived, I was in for another long wait. I didn't mind because it was the first time since leaving home that I felt safe enough to relax. When I first arrived, the waiting room was packed with people from all over the country. By the time I was finally called in to see the doctor, there were only two people left in the waiting room.

The doctor was kind, but stern and very businesslike. After a talk in his office, I had a thorough examination. When I was called back into his office, I received a tremendous blow. The doctor told me he required one year of hormone treatment prior to surgery. He assumed—erroneously—that I'd already had the treatment.

There was no way I could have known that such treatment was required. I had not gone the usual route in preparation for the surgery, and I had no doctor back home advising me. None of the doctors in Atlanta with whom I'd been in contact believed that the surgery was even possible.

The doctor was very regretful and I was in a terrible state. All I could think was, *I can't go back home without the surgery and I can't stay here!*

The doctor excused himself for a few minutes. When he returned, he told me that, since I had traveled such a great distance, perhaps he could do the first phase of the surgery. He explained that if he did do surgery now, he would remove the testicles and do some groundwork for the remaining surgery. He cautioned me not to get my hopes up, emphasizing again how important it was to have the hormone treatment prior to surgery.

He examined me again and then sent me to a barn-like building across the street for lab tests. When I returned to his office, I was ushered into an examining room and given four shots. The doctor talked to me again, and told me that I had a thyroid condition that prohibited immediate surgery. He told me to come back the next day and promised to give me his decision at that time. His expression gave me little hope.

I asked if he knew of a better hotel where I could stay for the night. He asked the receptionist to get me a room in a motel on the outskirts of town. It was located across from the bull ring, and compared to the one where I'd stayed the previous night, it was Heaven. It was called Motel Country Club, and I had a two-room suite at a cost of only seven dollars per night. But, I was so unhappy, I couldn't enjoy it. I was afraid that the doctor would not do the surgery, and I cried most of the night.

By the time morning came, I was convinced that if he didn't do the surgery, I would not leave Tijuana alive. There would be no point.

Back in his office the next day, the doctor must have sensed my desperation. He gave me the good news that I would be admitted to the hospital the following day, Sunday. I would be treated for the thyroid problem and then have the surgery on Monday of the following week. He dismissed me with a smile and said "I'll see you tomorrow."

As I stepped out of his office, a nurse said, "Come this way please," and gave me more injections.

I spent the night in the same motel, and had dinner in the motel restaurant, which was very nice. The food was delicious and a guitarist was strolling about. I was much more relaxed but I kept thinking, *with my kind of luck, something else will probably go wrong!*

The next morning, I entered the hospital without incident. It was a very small but modern facility. My room had sliding glass doors opening to a private patio, but I never once went outside. Soon after I checked in, I had a very good meal, and the first of countless injections. I had never seen such big needles, and the dosage was such that it seemed to take two minutes to complete each injection. I don't know what medication they were administering to me, but I could taste it immediately. I had so many shots that, by the time I left the hospital, my arms looked like pin cushions.

Finally, after thirteen horrible years of searching for a solution, I let myself believe it was really going to happen. I still had several days to go before the surgery—the days the doctor said would be required to treat my thyroid condition. I spent my time writing letters, watching television, and thinking. I had to deal with the fact that my change-of-sex would not be complete. I decided that when I went home, I would tell no one at what stage I was at in the change. I knew that if I shared the secret with even one person, I would not be in complete control of it.

I was very surprised to discover that hardly anyone in Tijuana spoke English. Only one nurse in the hospital spoke English, and I didn't see her until the second week of my hospitalization. My doctor was the only person I could talk to, and he was only there a few minutes each day.

On Wednesday night, February 5th, the doctor stopped in and informed me that I would be having surgery the following morning. He had purposely kept the information from me until then so I would remain as calm as possible. Shortly after he left, a burly woman came in to prepare me for surgery. She seemed very unconcerned, singing all the while she was working.

The next morning, when I awakened, I was still groggy from the pill I had been given the night before, but I was aware that I was being moved. Once I was in the operating room, the nurses coiled me up, wrapped my arms around my legs, and gave me a shot in my spine. The burning sting of the needle brought me out of my haze. I wasn't coherent enough to understand what was happening, and thought I was being mistreated. Furious, I yelled out, "Somebody stuck a needle in my back!"

A man said "Shut up and be still."

I felt the needle again and then nothing.

Back in my room, I awoke in excruciating pain. The catheter and the surgery were not at all compatible. I begged the doctor to remove the catheter. He told me that he would remove it in a few days, and explained that it was very important that my bandages not get wet. The night was painfully long and the shots for pain provided very little relief. The next morning I again pleaded with the doctor to remove the catheter. He said that he might do so that afternoon.

By the time he arrived that afternoon, I didn't think I could stand it a minute longer. I was ready to battle.

He agreed to remove the catheter but warned me again that the bandages must not get wet.

Now that the catheter was gone, the pain was not so bad. I had a good night's sleep, and the next morning I felt pretty good. After breakfast, I requested a telephone. It was the first time I had talked with my parents since they had received my letter informing them of my intentions. Our conversation was brief but pleasant. Their questions were confined to concern about how I was feeling and when was I coming home. Mother told me I had received quite a lot of mail, and I was anxious to see the mail.

I had to tell her I was in Mexico—not Los Angeles, as I had led them to believe. I gave her my address and asked that she share it with no one. It was more than a week before I received the first batch of letters. The following pages are the content of some of those letters from family, friends, and coworkers:

January 31, 1969

Dear J. C.,

Received your letter yesterday and want you to know to begin with that we still love you. Our relationship will be the same. Instead of being my favorite nephew, you will be my favorite niece. I will respect your wishes and not talk of the past, but hope we can talk of the present and future freely. I think this would be good. I hope you will write me when you are having the operation. Are you working now and will you continue to work at the same place?

I know as close as you have always been to your mother that you will continue to be. I realize that this transition period will be difficult for you and your family, but be assured my prayers are with you. I have known that you were not happy for some time and I trust you will find real happiness now.

I hope I have not been one of the ones to hurt you through the years but if so, please forgive me as it was not intentional. I will always respect you for being your true self and the Being that God made you. Hope to hear from you soon.

Love,

Lutrelle (Aunt)

✿ ✿ ✿

January 31, 1969

Dearest J.C.,

I have never been very good at expressing myself, but I want you to know and believe me, this comes from the bottom of my heart, to me you are still the same person you have always been. I love you as much now as ever and I think you know you have always been one of my favorite people. I would consider it a pleasure to have you in my home anytime. We have always had fun and I hope we will continue to do so. J.C., this is how we all feel. Please know that we are very happy for you.

Love, Aunt Emma

✿ ✿ ✿

February 9, 1969

Dear J.C.;

I hope you are doing alright. You have an ordeal in front of you. You needn't have worried about Billy and me accepting you or being embarrassed. You know us better than that. We'll stand behind you all the way.

It took a lot of courage to do what you are doing and I hope that afterwards everything will work out alright for you. I'm only sorry that you had to go through all this by yourself. I know it would have helped if you could have talked to someone.

Your mother says that you have nice surroundings where you are. That helps. If there is anything else you need that we can send you, let us know.

Everyone seems to be taking it alright. I don't believe that you will have too hard a time in that respect when you come back. If there is anything I can do for you before you are ready to come back, let me know. I will close for now; will write again soon. The boys are fine.

Georgia (Sister-in-law)

✿ ✿ ✿

February 11, 1969

Dear J.C.;

I got your letter. I was happy to hear from you and I think this is the wisest thing you could have done for yourself. I hope life will be happy for you.

J.C., please come to see me when you come home. You will always be welcome.

Love,

Ollie (Family Friend)

✿ ✿ ✿

January 30, 1969

Dear J.C.;

Thank you for giving us a chance to let you know how we feel. Mother called me shortly after she received your letter. I cried when I read it. Not because of the change you will make; but because you have suffered while we were happy. You asked us not to feel sorry for you. I couldn't, even if you felt sorry for yourself, which I know you do not by what was in your letter. I am happy for you. Now, as you say, you will have a chance to be your true self.

J. C., we don't realize how much we take for granted until someone we love suffers. I know I can't feel the hurt and anguish you have gone through; but I respect you very much. Very few people have ever had to carry such a burden and never let it show.

You are such a sweet person. Most people would be bitter; especially if you suffer because of someone's thoughtlessness.

It will take time for some to see you differently. But, time is a wonderful thing; it makes the past fade – all that matters is the present.

Again, thanks for giving me the chance to let you know I am for you all the way. If you have time, I would like to hear from you.

Love,

Jean (Cousin)

✧ ✧ ✧

February 10, 1969

Dear One;

No, we were not greatly surprised to receive your letter. In fact, we had mentioned something like that to each other. Not because we thought you were a "freak" or something but simply we were concerned that you did not and never did seem contented in your life.

Your letter has certainly not changed our feelings for you. You are part of our family and we love you. We are certainly not embarrassed about you. I won't say that we may not have awkward seconds the next time we see you, but it will not be because we do not love you or that we are ashamed of you. In fact, we were just a little hurt that you did not come with your folks to see us last summer. I hope it was not because we have hurt you in some way. We have never intended too. If either of us have, we ask you now to forgive us.

I'm not asking you how your folks have accepted this, but since you gave us a box number we assume you are not at home with them. But, I would like them to know that it does not change our feelings for you or for them.

Please let us know if there is any way we can help you. Do not be too proud or anything to ask for help if you need it. We can pray for your life to be fulfilled if we can't do anything else.

I'm writing this for all our family. We have not explained this to the children but I know they will understand.

I will close for now. I hope you will see in this letter what is in our hearts. Please let us hear from you real soon and let us know about you.

Julian and Edna (Uncle and Aunt)

✧ ✧ ✧

February 12, 1969

Dear J. C.;

We received your letter and J. C., I don't quite understand everything but no matter what your problem is; we will understand and you know we will always accept you, love you and never be embarrassed with you. We have always thought you are one of the finest people in the whole world. We always will. J.C., when you can we want you to come and visit us for as long as you can. I mean every word I have written you. Let us hear from you real soon.

All our love,

Your Aunt Pansy

✧ ✧ ✧

February 3, 1969

Dear J.C.;

Just a few lines to let you know I am thinking of you. J.C., it doesn't matter what happens; you are the same lovely boy you always was. You always thought of me and I love you; you have been such a good boy. I hope to see you again soon. I love you very much.

Love,

Granny

✵ ✵ ✵

February 3, 1969

Dear J. C.;

We received your letter today and we were very pleased to hear from you. We are proud you confided in us and trust us as your friends. You need not worry about us accepting you, for we understand and pray you will have a much happier life.

We never had any occasion to ever question your life; to us you are a number A-1 person. We think so much of you, your mother and father.

I have discussed it with your mother and they both are alright. I feel sure J.C., God is with you and your parents. I know it will be a big adjustment, but with your courage and the help of our Lord, miracles can be performed.

We are certainly thinking of you and if we can help you or your parents, please feel free to ask us. May God bless and be with you.

Sincerely,

Mr. and Mrs. Green (neighbors)

✲ ✲ ✲

January 19, 1969

Dear J. C.,

I'm sorry I have taken so long to reply to your letter, but needless to say – I was shocked.

J. C., why didn't you confide in someone long before now? I would have been glad to keep your secret and surely it would have helped to talk about it. I know you must have told someone of your plans – at least I hope that you did because I don't know how you could have stood not telling someone.

I wouldn't think of saying anything to your parents. I can imagine the shock that they must have expressed when they found out – or did they already know? J.C., I hope that when you do return to Atlanta; if that is your final plan, that we can openly discuss all that has happened. But knowing you as I do, I doubt if you will want to discuss it. I hope that this is not the case.

I believe that your transition will be difficult and I will do whatever is possible to help you through this period.

My personal opinion is that coming back to Atlanta may be extremely difficult for you because people will talk and many will try to make things hard for you. I'm sure that you have been advised about this many times and will do whatever the doctors feel is best for you, I hope.

I don't know whether this (the operation) is done frequently or not, but I have never heard of it before. I can imagine the legal aspects of it and the problems you must have faced. I must say that you have more courage than I would ever have.

I suppose that I have gone on about this long enough. I do wish you the best of luck and hope to see you as soon as possible. Please let me know how the operation comes out.

Benny (coworker)

✼ ✼ ✼

February 4, 1969

Hi;

Well, hope you are taking life easy and enjoying yourself. Still same old grind here. Lots of people are asking about you. You know you have lots of friends here and will always have them as I believe they are true friends.

J.C., please forgive me if I have ever done anything to hurt you; I did not have any idea that anything was wrong. I love you as I would my own child and wish the best of everything for you. Maybe we can have some more of our talks at my desk during lunch.

J. C., the reason I didn't want you to get out on your own was that I thought you had always been protected at home and I just didn't want anyone to hurt you when you got out in the world as they do.

Please take me in heart and forgive me if I have ever done anything to hurt you as I will always love you as my own. Write soon.

Love you.

Thelma Holloway (coworker)

☆ ☆ ☆

February 5, 1969

Hi J.C.;

It just doesn't seem the same around here without you. They are working the stew out of the others in your department. Every now and then I see Robert and some girl come up to get the transmittals from near Maggie.

Seems like one day Mr. Bowles called up the China Department and wanted a special order written for a replacement. When told "they were always written by J.C.", he said "we don't have time for that now." It tickled me because it showed how much work you did.

By the way, I told Catherine I was writing you; she said be sure and tell you she and Mrs. Griffin certainly missed you. I'm here at the office writing this and I better be careful. I've already been seen eating at my desk this morning and that is taboo now. It come from topside I understand. Well I better get back to work.

Best regards,

Ruth Cato (coworker)

✵ ✵ ✵

Hi Hon;

We got your letters this morning and mine was confiscated by Mr. Benson, however not before it was read. It irritated me no end. We have been forbidden to tell anyone what was in my letter, but I have told a couple of people that I know are your friends.

Of course you know Gunnin cried but you will find this hard to believe; Robert has cried all day.

You know you and I will always be friends and I believe the others feel the same way. This is going to take some adjusting by your family and friends as well as yourself, so don't be too hard on us if we say the wrong thing sometimes. All any of us want is for you to be happy.

Robert was in such a daze, he told Mr. Bowles that he had three trucks of layaway and didn't know what he did with them. Mr. Bowles told him that he had already worked them.

Mr. Bowles is trying to get your check released. I don't know if he succeeded or not, he won't tell us anything.

Has your mother told you that I'm picking up your mail for you? It worked out better that way. No one but Holloway knows I'm in touch with your parents. You and I have always discussed things we wouldn't discuss with anyone else. Can't you write me a few details as to what is going on out there? You know I worry about you.

Take care and remember we all love you.

Roberson (coworker)

☆ ☆ ☆

Needless to say, I was quite pleased with the acceptance expressed in these letters. However, not everyone who received a letter from me responded. I was concerned that the absence of responses to my letter meant that those people had chosen to disassociate themselves from me. I was disappointed, but I didn't dwell on it. As time went by, I would receive a letter from almost everyone to whom I had written.

I was feeling pretty good, and the last few days in the hospital were spent making plans. First, I had to decide on a name. I had considered several, and it was a difficult decision. I finally chose Phoebe. Then, I placed my first order from the mail order catalog I had brought with me on the trip. I was five feet, ten inches tall so I thought I should not wear three inch heels, I ordered two pairs of two inch heels. Ordering ladies apparel from a catalog was something I had longed to do for years, and it felt really good.

My stitches were removed on Thursday and the doctor discharged me from the hospital on Sunday. He told me that, as soon as I returned home, I must see an endocrinologist in New York, who would prescribe my hormone therapy. He explained that the endocrinologist would be the one to determine when I was ready for my second surgery.

I left the hospital early on Sunday morning. The walk from the taxi to the border was very tiring. There was a long line and my luggage was very heavy. By the time I reached the guard, I was exhausted. He asked me a few questions about my reason for being in Mexico, and the duration of my stay. I told him I had been in Mexico for three days, visiting friends. Apparently, my story didn't sound very convincing because he became suspicious and took me inside.

Another guard asked me more questions—and then asked me to take off my coat. One of the guards turned my arm to show the other guard and said "needle marks." They bombarded me with questions about the needle marks and demanded to know where I had been before coming to Mexico. They persisted in questioning me until I finally admitted to having sex-change surgery.

I was taken into a small room, where they asked me to undress. I was given a very thorough body search. I had no idea of the places people hide narcotics to bring across the border. When it was over, one of the guards said, "I'm sorry, I was only doing my job." Needless to say, it was an experience I will never forget.

For my journey home, my round-trip ticket was from Los Angeles to Atlanta, so I took a taxi to the San Diego Airport and flew to Los Angeles. When I reached the Los Angeles airport, I called my parents and told them I would be home the next morning. And, then another long wait. I arrived in Atlanta early on Monday morning, and my father was there to meet me. There was no tension, and our conversation was casual and relaxed. Everything between us was the same as it had always been. It was as if I'd never gone away.

When we arrived home, the first thing I saw was a "For Sale" sign in the front yard. My parents had the house for sale because they thought

I would want to move. I didn't—I was home and prepared to face everyone and everything all the way. The fact that my parents had a for-sale sign in the yard when I returned home after surgery says a lot about our relationship.

Mother met me at the door, hugged me, and told me how much she had missed me. She had breakfast ready and, as we ate, it seemed that we were all careful not to mention my surgery.

When the news spread among my relatives and others that I was home, the phone began ringing and continued into the night. I didn't see anyone that first day but my parents. A few relatives dropped by the next day. Everyone seemed to want to assure me that I had their support.

The order I had placed for the clothes and shoes had arrived before I got home. I didn't like the way the two inch heels looked and I wasn't comfortable walking in them.

I needed to call the doctor in New York and make an appointment. I didn't waste any time, setting up an appointment for Thursday of that week. I had much to do in a couple of days, and very little money. Prior to my trip to Mexico, I had obtained a credit card with Eastern Airlines, planning to use it to purchase my ticket to Los Angeles. As my luck would have it, Eastern didn't have a flight to Los Angeles. But, the credit card came in handy now, as I was able to use it for my trip to New York.

As it turned out, my last deed as J.C. was to purchase a ticket for myself as Phoebe. I would never again leave the house dressed as a male.

SEVEN

On Wednesday, Phoebe began to emerge, little by little. Three cousins came over to help with my transformation. It was awkward at first, but my cousins' presence and support made the transition easier. The procedure took all day. First, I put on a wig, and we sat around and talked. Then the makeup was applied, and finally the clothes. From head to toe, I was now Phoebe. It was time to venture out for my first outing— a shopping trip. My Aunt Mildred bought me three dresses.

The following day, I went to New York to see the doctor for my hormone prescription. Aunt Mildred, Aunt Lillie, and my cousin, Connie, accompanied me. It was the first time Phoebe had been out in the daylight. I had no way of gauging how believable I was, but I watched very closely, and didn't see anyone giving me second looks.

It was a fun day, and we had a lot of laughs. My relatives still thought of me as J. C. and many funny things happened. Once, my cousin asked her mother, "Where's your scarf?" Her mother replied "It's in J. C.'s purse." We all burst into laughter as she quickly looked to see if anyone had heard her.

During the next few weeks, I was constantly on the go. Everyone wanted to see me. Relatives and friends invited me for overnight visits. Occasionally when I was visiting one relative, another would just happen to stop by. It was obvious that they were just curious.

I was feeling well at that point, but I did have one problem—every time I sat down, I wet myself. One day while in downtown Atlanta, I glanced down and saw a big wet circle on my skirt. From then on, I made sure I was well protected from that embarrassment. That problem persisted until after the second operation.

By the middle of March, I was getting restless, and decided it was time for me to go back to work. When I went in to discuss returning to my old job, word spread like wildfire that I was in the store. I was followed everywhere I went. Most of the people I knew were happy to see me, but a few were not. When it came to light that I planned to return to my job, a movement was started to bar my return.

Store officials actually took a survey, asking women such questions as "What would you do if Phoebe asked you to go to the bathroom with her?"

One lady replied, "It depends on which way her toes are pointed." The implication was that a woman's feet would be pointed towards the stall door and a man's would be pointed towards the wall.

Three women were dead set against my return. I had a close working relationship with all three, so I was disappointed with them but I wasn't angry.

My supervisor, Mr. Bowles, was given the task of telling me I would not be allowed to return to my old job. When I let him know I could not accept that decision, he arranged an appointment for me to see a higher level official. That person tried to discourage me from returning by saying, "If you were allowed to return, you would be disruptive to the whole store! Not only that, you would continually be on display."

He said he felt sure I wouldn't want that, and pointed out that the transition would be much easier for me if I got a job somewhere else.

I disagreed. I felt strongly that, if I could face people at the store, where they knew me, I could face people anywhere. I had two more appointments, each time with a higher level official. Finally, on April 3rd, I was told by the personnel director that, as a result of my operation, I was unsuitable for the work I had been previously performing, and he had no other job in which to place me. In my mind, this set the precedent. I figured, *If the store doesn't want me to work there, no one else will, either!* I was very hurt.

March 1969 (First Photo as Phoebe)

On April 13th, I signed up to receive unemployment insurance. This provided me with forty-two dollars per week for six months. In order to continue receiving unemployment checks, I was required to consistently look for work. I went on many job interviews, but wherever I went, it was the same thing—once I revealed my history, the interview was over.

My parents told me to forget about getting a job until I had my next operation. I tried, but it was easier said than done. I spent some time visiting relatives and friends, but after a while, that got old.

While visiting one friend, she suggested taking me to her hairdresser. I let her shape my hair and cut bangs, but I wasn't comfortable with the haircut, and continued to wear wigs. Eventually, I started cutting my own hair, and have continued to do so.

On April 15th, I began keeping a diary. Here is my last comment of that day's entry: "Another can be added to the list of those who don't accept me. Still I have lost nothing." That entry was referring to an acquaintance of the friend who took me to the hairdresser.

I was constantly on the go, which was good for me, and quite a departure from my previous existence. When I wasn't on the go, I was bored. After all those years of seeking to solve my problems, I was now at a loss for something meaningful to do.

I had few social acquaintances, and the former gay coworker and his friend had friends who wanted to meet me. In fact, I met a lot of their friends, one of whom gave me a huge party to introduce me. That resulted in more invitations. Everyone was very nice and I was happy for the companionship, but after a while I realized that this wasn't where I needed to be. Gay men are not interested in women and I am not a lesbian. Clearly I was going to the wrong places. But I had lots of relatives and some friends, so I wasn't without people in my life.

All of a sudden, people began to confide in me. A number of people told me they were gay, and two married women told me they were bisexual. I didn't want to know these things, but I could understand the need to talk about such issues with someone they thought they could trust. They weren't wrong about that—their secrets were safe with me.

On May 3rd, I entered in my diary: "Today we came to Tifton to visit relatives. I haven't seen anyone here since my surgery. All seemed to accept me except two cousins. One of them did not exchange greetings with me, and I later learned that he did not know who I was. The other one was very cool, and gave me a look that indicated that the less he had to do with me, the better he would like it. I ignored him completely from that moment on and shall forever do so." (I have seen that particular cousin several times since then, and we are friendly.)

Mother and I often talked after daddy went to bed. One night she told me an uncle had told her and daddy that he didn't like J.C., but he loved Phoebe. J.C. didn't like him either but I loved him too. I think he thought J.C. was worthless – a lot of people thought that.

Once we were back from Tifton, I was on the go again. A high school biology class invited me to come in for a question and answer session, but I declined.

I was interviewed for a local television news program. Prior to the airing of the interview, the news anchor reported that the interviewer had called his interview with me "the most delicate interview of his career." I had hoped this interview would help make me old news faster, as the majority of people in the area where I lived would see it. No such luck; I continued to be news to one person or another. I had also hoped the interview might lead to a job, but that didn't happen either.

On June 2nd, 1969, I had my first kiss ever. I noted in my diary that it didn't seem obvious to the boy I was kissing that there was anything different about me. In July, I started going out of the house without a wig. But after trying to sleep in curlers, I really came to appreciate wigs. I enjoyed wearing a blond wig, especially while waiting for buses. Men driving by would blow their horns and whistle, and I was pleased to know they thought I was attractive.

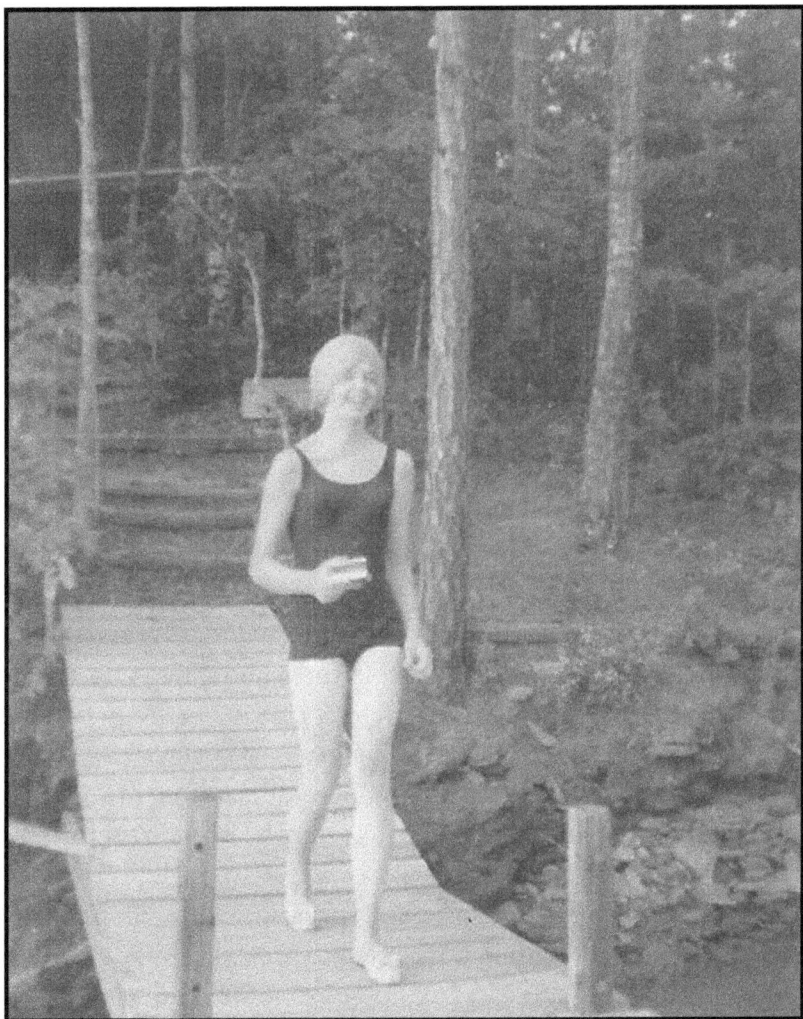

June 1969

I had my first cocktail when I was twenty-seven years old, and over the next couple of years, I had cocktails fairly often. I never thought I would get into the drinking scene, and my mother was very disappointed. After I had my surgery and became more social, I had more and more cocktails. If I went to a club, I would not be comfortable until after I'd had a couple of drinks, and it took more than that for me to feel relaxed enough to dance.

By the time August rolled around, I was bored and restless. Being on the go all the time was not the answer, and it solved nothing. Yet, I could do nothing really constructive until the surgery was complete. I had tried to find a job, but there seemed to be nothing I could do but wait. On August 24th, I wrote in my diary, *I will probably leave Atlanta after I complete my surgery. I can't get a job here.*

I began attending the First Baptist Church in Hapeville, and there were a lot of social activities as the holidays approached. I was acquainted with the minister's secretary, and soon was acquainted with the pastor and his family. They often picked me up to attend church functions. I was attending most services, and the pastor frequently visited me at home, as well. He thought that I was ready to join the church and I was seriously considering it—until he told me I would have to stand in front of the church congregation while he told them about me.

I didn't think anyone had the right to decide if I was fit to be a member of a church. God would not turn me away.

I told him I would have to think about it, but before his car left my driveway I knew I would never go through with it. I didn't return to the church for several months, and then only a few times.

For years, both before and after my surgery, my mother had tried to get me to go to church with her. I wanted to go with her, but I felt it was best for her if I didn't. Like it or not, there are some mean and judgmental religious people and I did not want my mother to overhear someone saying something hurtful about me. That would have hurt her and I would not have stood for that. I never told her why I didn't go.

On November 16th, I went back to New York to see Dr. Harry Benjamin. He gave me the good news that I was ready to have the final surgery. When I returned home, I wrote to Dr. Barbosa in Tijuana, and advised him that I was ready to come back to complete the surgery. By the time January came around, I had not heard from Dr. Barbosa, and I was becoming concerned. I had already paid him the full amount, and I began to fear that I might not hear from him again.

I wrote a second letter to him. I also wrote to the Georgia Office of Vital Records concerning changing my birth certificate. The following is their reply.

Dear Miss Smith:

We acknowledge receipt of your letters of December 2 and January 15 regarding your birth certificate. The certificate which is on file for you lists your name as James Cleveland Smith. Since the certificate lists your sex as male and this was not an error, it cannot be corrected except by court order. The Vital Records Chapter of the Georgia Health Code provides for the correction of records and the change of other records after adoption, legitimation, or other changes which the court deems advisable. The original certificates are not changed but an amendment is added to show what correction has been made in any case other than adoption or legitimation.

We will be glad to issue a certified copy of your birth certificate as it was registered when you were born. This certificate with documents showing the change in your status could be used when it is necessary for you to prove your identity and age. The fee for a copy is $1.00 payable in advance. We suggest that you call the office of the Clerk *of the Federal Court. They will be glad to give you any information needed to obtain a passport.*

We will be glad to have you call on us at any time we may assist you with matters pertaining to vital records.

Sincerely,

Miss Martha Patillo

Assistant Director, Vital Records Service

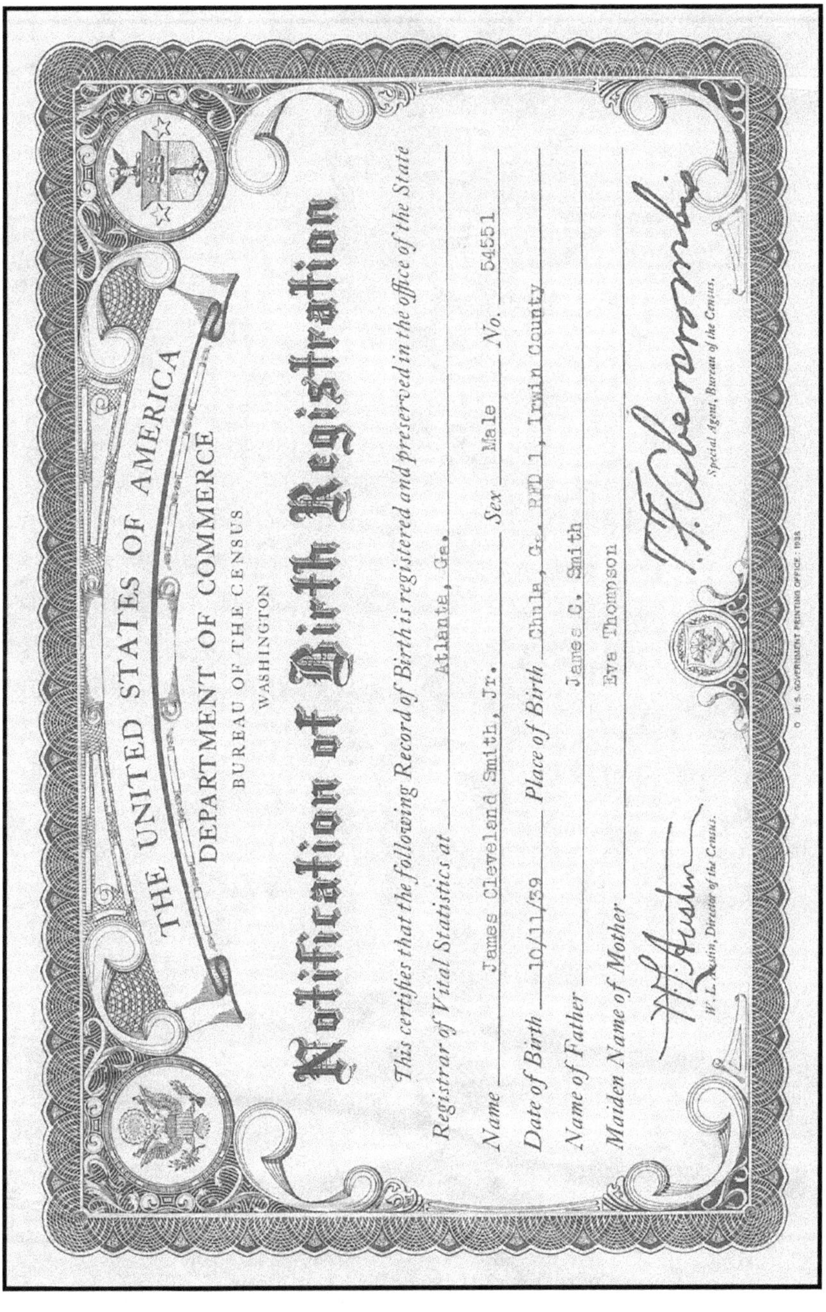

THE UNITED STATES OF AMERICA

DEPARTMENT OF COMMERCE

BUREAU OF THE CENSUS

WASHINGTON

Notification of Birth Registration

This certifies that the following Record of Birth is registered and preserved in the office of the State Registrar of Vital Statistics at Atlanta, Ga.

Name James Cleveland Smith, Jr. *Sex* Male *No.* 54551

Date of Birth 10/11/39 *Place of Birth* Chula, Ga., RFD 1, Irwin County

Name of Father James C. Smith

Maiden Name of Mother Eva Thompson

W. L. Austin, Director of the Census.

Special Agent, Bureau of the Census.

Original Birth Certificate

FULTON SUPERIOR COURT

ATLANTA JUDICIAL CIRCUIT

O R D E R

DEPARTMENT HUMAN RESOURCES

RE: CHANGE OF NAME AND SEX ON BIRTH CERTIFICATE

It appearing to the Court that JAMES CLEVELAND SMITH, JR. a male child was born on October 11, 1939. It further appearing to the Court that said JAMES CLEVELAND SMITH, JR., has had a trans-sexual operation and that said JAMES CLEVELAND SMITH, JR., as a result of said operation is now a female.

THEREFORE, it is the ORDER of this Court that the Department of Human Resources, the Director or Agent in charge of said department, is directed and ordered to change any and all records, and certificate of birth regarding JAMES CLEVELAND SMITH, JR., so that the name will read as follows: PHOEBE SMITH, FEMALE.

AND IT IS SO ORDERED THIS 6th DAY OF JUNE, 1974.

Charles A. Wofford

JUDGE CHARLES A. WOFFORD, A. J. C.

Court Order to Change Birth Certificate

B044014

CERTIFICATE OF BIRTH
GEORGIA DEPARTMENT OF PUBLIC HEALTH

State File No. 34551

DEPARTMENT OF COMMERCE
BUREAU OF THE CENSUS

Registrar's No.

1. Place of Birth

(a) County Irwin   Militia Dist. No.

2. Usual Residence of Mother

(a) State Georgia   (b) County Irwin

(b) City or Town Chula

(c) City or Town Chula

(c) Name of Hosp. or St. Address

(d) House No. & St. or R.F.D. & Box Route 1

(d) Length of Mother's Stay Before Delivery In Hosp.   Is This Community

Hour of Birth 5:20 A.M.

3. Full Name of Child   Phoebe Smith

4. Date of Birth October 11 yr 39

5. Sex Female   6. Twin or Triplet   Born 1st 2nd or 3rd   7. Full Term Pregnancy. If Not Give Months Gestation   8. Is Mother Married To Father of This Child? Yes

FATHER OF CHILD

MOTHER OF CHILD

9. Full Name James C. Smith

16. Maiden Name Eva Thompson

10. Color White   11. Age at Time of This Birth 24

17. Color White   18. Age at Time of This Birth 19

12. Birth Place of Father Fulton County, Georgia

19. Birth Place of Mother Tift County, Georgia

13. Usual Occupation Farmer

20. Usual Occupation Housewife

14. Industry or Business   15. Social Security No.

21. Industry or Business   22. Social Security No.

23. Was This Child Born Alive? Yes   24. Total No. of Children Born to This Mother 1

Born Alive (a) Now Living 1   Born Alive (b) Now Dead 0   Born (c) Dead 0

25. I. R.'s Own Signature   H. L. Layton

27. I hereby certify that I attended the birth of this child who was born on the date stated above. The personal information as given on this certificate was furnished by

26. Date Filed November 13, 1939   Date of Supplementary Report

Mr. Mrs. James C. Smith

SUPPLEMENTARY DATA NOT A PART OF LEGAL CERTIFICATE

Give Complications of Preg. or Labor.

Related to the child as Parents

Was 1% Silver Nitrate Solution Used in This Child's Eyes? Yes

Was This an Operative Delivery?

Attendant's Own Signature   D. B. Harrell M.D.

Was There a Birth Injury? Describe.

Attendant's P.O. Address Tifton, Georgia   Date Signed Oct. 12, 1939

Congenital Deformity?

New Birth Certificate

(In 1974, my birth certificate would finally be changed, thanks to a friend/coworker who was friends with a judge. She arranged for him to issue a court order to issue me a new birth certificate at no cost to me.)

On March 31st, 1970, the telegram finally arrived from Dr. Barbosa, directing me to arrive on April 11th. Surgery would be on April 13th. I had ten days to get everything in order. I called the Mexican Consulate and asked that they send me a tourist card (a border pass). I also wrote to the Motel in Tijuana and asked that they reserve a room for me for April 10th. I was both excited and afraid, and the time passed quickly. I didn't cherish the thought of returning to Mexico and the night before my departure, I didn't sleep at all.

When I reached San Diego, I called the motel in Tijuana. When I tried to confirm the reservation I'd requested by mail, I was told they had no vacancy. (I can't imagine why I didn't call and make the reservation.)

I got a room in a Ramada Inn in San Diego, checked in, and immediately went to bed. My plan was to take a nap, have a good dinner, and listen to the in-house entertainment. I knew it would be weeks before I enjoyed an outing of any kind. When I awoke, it was after 11:00 p.m. I called my parents to let them know I had arrived safely, and went back to sleep.

After breakfast the following morning, I took a taxi to the border. This time, I made sure I did everything right.. The guard took one copy of my tourist card, and told me to turn in the other copy as I was leaving Mexico.

Walking to the taxi felt very different this time. The only luggage I was carrying was my cosmetic case, and I was wearing the dress I would wear on my return trip. I shared a taxi with four other people. I was not comfortable with that; but when the others got out of the taxi, I was more uncomfortable. The driver started flirting with me, saying that I was a very pretty American lady. I thanked him for the compliment, but I was afraid to smile.

EIGHT

This time I didn't have to wait long to see the doctor. When he came in he seemed pleased with my appearance. After a brief conversation, he sent me to check into the hospital. I was relieved that he sent his porter to accompany me to the hospital, although the porter didn't utter a word during the trip to the hospital, or go inside with me when we arrived.

I went up to the girl at the desk, and handed her the papers the doctor had given to me. She said something in Spanish and pointed to a waiting room, which was packed with people. During the whole time I was sitting there, I never heard a word of English. Two hours later, I was still sitting there. I went back to the desk, but the girl who had taken my papers was nowhere to be found. The girl who had replaced her did not understand a word I said.

I went back to the waiting room, and before long, I started getting hungry and irritated. I went back to the front desk, and fortunately, the first girl had returned. Her expression let me know she had forgotten about me. She wasted no time in getting me to my room.

I had a good meal and a good night's sleep. In the morning, I was awakened by a nurse who came in to give me an injection. Later, the doctor stopped by and told me that I would go to surgery at eight o'clock the next morning.

That afternoon was miserable. I couldn't get interested in anything. I tried reading and watching television, but I had trouble concentrating. I did write some letters. Then, I called my parents to let them know I would call them as soon as I was able to after surgery.

After my evening meal, a woman came in to prep me for surgery. She shaved me and left. I hated enemas, but I remembered having one before the first surgery, and knew I was supposed to have one now. So, I pressed the call button for a nurse, and tried to explain to her that I had not had an enema. None of the nurses on duty spoke English, and I couldn't make any of them understand.

A nurse brought my knock-out pill to me that night, but before I took it I attached a note to my pillow. I wrote, "I did not have an enema." I was hoping someone would see it the next morning before I went in to surgery.

I was expecting to be as groggy the next morning as I had been the last time, but I was awake when they took me to the operating room. After receiving my spinal injection, I got onto the operating table by myself. I was strapped into the same position they use with women who are giving birth. I opened my eyes once, and saw several curious people looking between my legs. I was embarrassed and angry, but didn't say anything—I just closed my eyes again.

When I opened my eyes again, I was back in my room, and immediately put my hand between my legs. The doctor was standing by my bed, and told me that it was over and everything was going to be fine. I slept most of the rest of that day and night, and much of the next day.

Oddly enough, my primary source of discomfort wasn't the surgical area—it was my left foot. For some reason, it was cold, numb, and very uncomfortable. I worried that something might have gone wrong, but the doctor assured me that everything would be fine.

The second day after surgery, I was acutely aware of the ordeal I had been through. When the doctor came by that day, he told me he would remove the catheter and stitches eleven days after surgery, and I would be on a liquid diet until that time. I was told to lie on my back and keep as still as possible.

On the third day, they lowered the rails on my bed. That night, I dreamed that I had forgotten my cousin Connie's wedding. When I awoke, I was sitting in a chair, removing the catheter. I was horrified when I realized what I had done, and terrified that I might have really messed up. It was a struggle to get back into bed. The movement caused agonizing pain.

When I pressed the call button for a nurse, God was with me. The English speaking nurse I had seen the first time I was hospitalized answered the call. She was very concerned over what I had done, but was reluctant to call my doctor because she along with everyone else at the hospital was afraid of him. The doctor was very stern and not friendly with the staff. The nurse pushed the catheter a little bit, and I felt like I was being cut. I stopped her because I was afraid that she might be tearing me inside.

My bed had not been changed since my surgery, and the note was still attached to my pillow. The nurse saw it and exclaimed, "Oh! You want enema!" I assured her I didn't.

I dreaded seeing the doctor the next day. When I told him what I had done, he angrily asked, "Why you do that?" He didn't seem at all interested in why or how it had happened. He pushed the catheter in and put my bed rails back up. The catheter was taped to my leg to keep it from moving. The part that touched my leg had already burned a two-inch area of skin on my leg, so he changed the tape site. By the time I left the hospital, I had two such burns because infection had caused the temperature of the urine in the catheter tube to be so high.

During my stay in the hospital, I jotted down some notes for my diary. On April 17th, I wrote:

> *Surgery was Monday morning. The pain is agonizing. Last night another patient sneaked in to see me. The English speaking nurse told her that I was there. Her surgery was seven days before mine. She told me that, if she had known how bad it was going to be, she wouldn't have done it.*

> *The doctor had used skin from her leg to line her vagina. Skin from the penis had been used for mine. Her stitches had*

been removed that day, seven days after surgery. I thought I must have misunderstood the doctor when he told me that my stitches would be removed eleven days after surgery.

Also on the 17th, I wrote:

Mother and Daddy called tonight (they called every day after I had surgery). I told them how much pain I was experiencing, and immediately regretted telling them. They will just worry even more.

On Sunday, my new friend went home. I'd only seen her three times, but I missed her. I asked the doctor if he would remove my stitches the next day, which would have been seven days after surgery. He replied "No…Thursday," which was four days away. I was so miserable.

On Tuesday, the pain was unbearable. The doctor said that part of the pain was caused from the stitches pulling as I healed. The shots I had been receiving didn't ease the pain, and that afternoon, I was given morphine. What a relief! I actually felt good. I was given morphine the next day, as well.

Finally the big day was here. I was taken back to the operating room, and placed in the same position as for surgery. After the catheter, packing and stitches were removed, the doctor inserted a part of a machine in the opening and turned it on briefly. I don't know what it was, I didn't see it; but I felt it. I didn't ask him why and he didn't give me a reason for doing it.

Afterwards, I was taken back to my room. I was totally exhausted, and glad to be rid of the catheter. I knew that meant I would now have to go to the bathroom. I still had a lot of pain and I was bleeding. I had to wear a sanitary napkin to catch the blood. When I went to the bathroom for the first time, I was in for quite a shock. Urine went everywhere but where it was supposed to go, ending up all over me and the bathroom floor.

The next day, the doctor explained that I had an infection, but when it cleared up, I would have no further problems.

I asked him when I could go home, and he replied, "We'll see." That evening, I had a real meal, breaking the liquids-only diet I'd been on for eleven days.

The following day, the doctor inserted a tube in the opening. It was painful, and I bled quite a bit. This was done to prevent shrinkage. I was informed that I would have to continue this procedure after I returned home.

On Saturday, the doctor asked me if I thought I would be strong enough to go home the following day. It was all I could do to go to the bathroom, but I was ready to get out of there and go home. I called the airport and made a reservation for a flight leaving San Diego at 7:50 a.m.

When I awoke the next morning, it was raining. I was afraid the rain would prevent me from leaving the hospital, but by the time I was ready to go, the rain had stopped. I dreaded crossing the border. The memory of the last time was still quite vivid.

I needn't have worried. It was very early when I arrived at the border, and there was only one guard outside at the crossing point. When I handed him the remaining part of my tourist card, he said, "We don't need that. But, you ought to mail it back to the Mexican officials, in case you come back to Mexico."

It was 8:05 in the morning when I reached the airport, and I had missed the flight. There would not be another one until four o'clock in the afternoon. By now, I wished I had never left the hospital. It was too soon for so much activity. I'd been lying in a hospital bed for two weeks, and this was too much all at once.

Standing was painful, and sitting was worse. I desperately needed to lie down, but there was no place to stretch out. I was in a lot of pain and feeling weak. I was beginning to bleed and I was afraid I might faint. I wondered if I should tell someone about my predicament, but decided against it.

Somehow I made it through the day, spending most of the time in the restroom. When I arrived in Atlanta I was in so much pain I could barely walk. My parents met me at the airport, and I spent the next few days in bed, getting up only to go to the bathroom. Using the tube was torture. During the first few days, it often took me over an hour to insert it.

On May 5th, I went to see my doctor in Atlanta. He said that I was healing well, and the surgeon had done an excellent job.

On May 11th, I wrote in my diary:

I feel pretty good now. I'm not completely healed, but I am progressing well.

On May 26th, I wrote:

Since my last entry, I have had a minor setback. I had to see my doctor, who said I had developed areas of proud flesh and had become very raw. Also, tonight some boys rode by my house shouting "Phoebe, baby!" My main concern was that it would upset my parents.

One afternoon while sitting outside, I heard a small child saying something to me. I had to listen to be sure I heard him correctly. He was saying, "Hey lady-man, lady-man!" His mom heard him and called him inside. The next time she saw me, she told me he knew who I was. He told her, "I know him by his nose." He never said anything to me again.

Another day, I was walking down the sidewalk and passed a woman who lived across the street from me. We had never met. I smiled and wanted to speak, but her wide-eyed stare silenced me. She never took eyes off me. For more than twenty years, I lived across the street from her and we never did speak. After that, I pretty much avoided my neighbors except the ones who lived on either side of us.

It was the end of June before I really felt well. I was going out quite a lot by then, and was quite pleased with myself.

One Saturday afternoon in June, I received a call from a cousin with whom I had a close relationship. She was out with an ex-husband and a friend of his, and was calling to see if I wanted to join them. I told her that I would, but she would have to tell them about my surgery. If they were okay with it, I would join them. I fully expected her to call back and say, "No, it was not okay."

When she called back, she said, "Everything is fine! No problem."

When they picked me up, I was pleasantly surprised. Mel, the friend of my cousin's ex-husband was very handsome and likeable. We had a very good time, and when he asked for my phone number, I was glad to give it to him. As the night was winding down, we stopped to eat. I ordered and then went to the restroom.

When I returned to the table, the atmosphere was totally different. Mel was extremely angry. So was my cousin's ex-husband. My cousin had told her ex-husband about my surgery, but he hadn't told Mel until I went to the restroom. Mel was angry and my cousin's ex-husband was drunk and belligerent. I didn't eat, and I'm not sure whether anyone else did or not. I was very frightened.

When we left, they drove me deep into some woods. The men were pushing me and telling me what they were going to do to me. I thought they were going to kill me. I had heard about transsexuals who were murdered by men when they learned they were out with a transsexual.

Finally, I said, "If you're going to kill me, go ahead and get it over with!"

I tried to explain to Mel that I was told that he knew about my surgery, and I was under the impression he did not have a problem with it.

He yelled, "I didn't know anything about no damn surgery!" After a while, he calmed down. But my cousin's ex-husband was still in a drunken state, and refused to take me home. They did let me call my parents to tell them I wouldn't be home until the following day. We spent the night at a motel just outside Atlanta, and the next morning they couldn't apologize enough.

They took me home and I never saw Mel or my cousin's ex-husband again. Mel did call several times. I liked him and believed he was the only one who told the truth about who knew what and when they were told.

NINE

As I mentioned, my job search after my first surgery yielded disappointing results so I postponed it. When I began looking for a job after my second surgery, I contacted the counselor at the state employment office. I told him I wanted to be open and honest with my history. He didn't think it was a good idea, but he went along with it, and tried to find something for me.

No one would even interview me. One man told the counselor, "I ain't touching that one!" I did get an interview with *The Atlanta Journal* but to no avail.

I was offered a job at the Regency Hyatt Hotel—but they rescinded the employment offer the very next day. Someone from the hotel called and told me that a vice president didn't think it was in the best interest of the hotel for me to work there.

One afternoon in the summer of 1970, a casual friend called. She told me that her husband was going out of town for the night, and he'd suggested she invite me over to spend the night. I had visited the two of them previously and thought nothing of the invitation. We went out to dinner with her daughter and her family.

On the way home, we picked up a bottle of liquor. After a couple of drinks, I went to the restroom. When I returned, I found her sitting in a kitchen chair with her feet in the chair and knees wide apart. She wanted me to touch her.

I was so shaken up, I went into my bedroom and locked the door. I tossed and turned all night, unable to sleep. When I came out the next morning, I could see that she was distraught over what she had done. She begged me to forgive her and pleaded with me not to tell anyone. I promised her I wouldn't tell, and I never did. After that incident, we spoke a couple of times by phone, but the conversation was strained. I never saw her again. She is now deceased.

Despite the letter I'd received from the Georgia Office of Vital Records, I decided to check with Legal Aid to see if they could help me get my birth certificate changed. They were very interested initially, but ultimately told me they could do nothing because I lived with my father and his income would disqualify me from eligibility for Legal Aid.

So, I checked with the Equal Employment Commission about the possibility of getting re-hired at my old job. The Commission told me that, if I had contacted them within ninety days of the store's refusal to reinstate me, they could have helped me. They also told me I might have a case against Vocational Rehabilitation, but they had no jurisdiction in that area.

I finally concluded that, if I wanted to get a job, I was going to have to stop being so open and honest. I felt like I'd been too open and honest to suddenly do an about-face, but I could see no other way.

In terms of official records, Phoebe did not yet exist. I had no birth certificate, no school or work record—nothing. I didn't know how far I would be able to progress in my employment search, but I had come too far to quit now.

I took a State Merit test and it wasn't long until I was receiving notices to come in for an interview. My first interview was with Miss Patillo in Vital Records, the lady who had responded to my letter concerning changing my birth certificate. I was scheduled to go back for a second interview, but before the time came for that appointment I accepted another job at a lower classification, in Disease Investigation. At least I was in.

On October 21ˢᵗ, I wrote in my diary:

I am to report for work on November 2ⁿᵈ. They will refer me to the Employment Health Department for a physical. I called them and told them I was scheduled to have a physical from my personal doctor and could this examination serve for their records as well. I was told that would be acceptable.

On November 8ᵗʰ, I entered in my diary:

I'm working now and I don't like it…

On November 16ᵗʰ, I wrote:

I still don't like it, though I will keep it for now. As far as I know, they don't know anything about me. I hope I don't come unglued when they find out.

When I first started the job, I made a decision not to become friendly with my coworkers. This made me appear cold and unfriendly. Ironically, this also made me intriguing. By the first of December I had relaxed a little, and become friendly with the ladies with whom I worked. It was unavoidable—unless I wanted to come across as rude. They were too nice to ignore, and I really did like them.

On December 1ˢᵗ one of the ladies in the office invited me to be her overnight guest. It turned out she had some interesting news—there was a man about my age in the office, and he was interested in me. This news delighted me because I found this man attractive. It also scared me. I didn't think it would be wise for me to get involved with someone at work. So, I was not friendly towards him.

A few weeks later he relocated. As much as I'd wanted to get to know him, I knew it was best for me (and him) that he had left. I put it out of my mind. I was so surprised when he showed up at the office Christmas party. The next day I entered in my diary: *I'm disappointed with the end result of the party. I wanted us to become better acquainted. We stared at one another half of the evening. He asked me to dance. I refused; I had not danced before. We were partners in a game.*

One day, the lady who had invited me to spend the night at her home asked me to go home with her the following evening. I told her I would. Then, she asked me if I minded if she had her hair fixed on the way home. It was fine with me until our conversation revealed that her hairdresser was the lady who had styled my hair when I was first making my transition. The hairdresser knew all about me, so I couldn't risk seeing her again.

Of course, I declined my coworker's invitation. Even so, I worried that my friend might mention my name to the hairdresser, who could have unwittingly spilled the beans.

Another time, this same friend and I were in Rich's, the store where I had worked for ten years. I mentioned that I wanted to go to the cosmetics department. She said, "Oh good, a girl in my square dance club works in that department!" She told me the girl's name, and I knew her too—quite well, in fact. I made sure we didn't have time to go by the cosmetics department, and I never visited that store with her again.

One day, I was approached by a lady who was temporarily housed in our offices. She worked in Medicaid, and offered me a job as her secretary. I was hired without an interview. Before I transferred out of my old job, a new male employee joined the team.

I started the new job on May 1st, 1971.

Also in May, I attended a four-day convention. Also in attendance were two female coworkers from my previous job, and the male employee who had joined the unit before my transfer. On the second day of the convention, one of the ladies I was with mentioned this man to me. She said, "He told me he has something to tell me about you. What could he know about you?"

I told her I didn't know. It upset me but I didn't let it spoil my trip. I was quite popular at the convention, and had two dates. One was with a health official from the state of South Carolina, who was friends with the president of our convention—the Georgia Public Health Association. The other date was with an exhibitor.

I also met an Atlanta television news person at the convention and while we didn't have a date, we did dance several times. We stayed in touch for years. Sometimes he would call to go out between the six o'clock and eleven o'clock news programs.

When we returned home, I became uneasy about what the man might have told my friend. She didn't behave any differently around me, so after a while, I stopped worrying about it.

During the summer, an organization interested in helping transsexuals contacted me. They wanted to know if I could meet with pre-op transsexuals in the Atlanta area. I agreed to do so, knowing what it would have meant to me when I was pre-op. A psychologist joined us as a moderator. There wasn't a very good turnout, so after the fourth meeting, we decided against further meetings.

Meanwhile, my cousins and I frequented a popular dance club, and I dated several men I met there. One night, I was out partying with one of them, and we wound up at his apartment. We kept partying and wound up in bed.

It was my first time, and I wanted to see if he could determine anything different about me. He uttered something about my "virgin ass." The act was very painful, but I didn't have any doubts about myself the next time.

One night in the spring of 1971, I was in bed when I received a call. I did not know the man who was calling, but he knew my name, where I lived and where I worked. He told me he was on his way to pick me up and when I told him I was in bed with curlers in my hair, he said, "That's alright, be ready."

He told me if I didn't go with him, he would show up at my job the next day. I couldn't risk that so I got dressed. I didn't want to alarm my parents and I also didn't want him to show up at my job. I wasn't scared, I was angry.

He picked me up and we rode around and talked for about an hour. He would not tell me who gave him my information. I knew it had to be one of two people, and I was pretty sure I knew which one. He insisted we were going to be friends and see each other. The next day he showed up at my office anyway. That was the very thing I was hoping to avoid by agreeing to see him the night before.

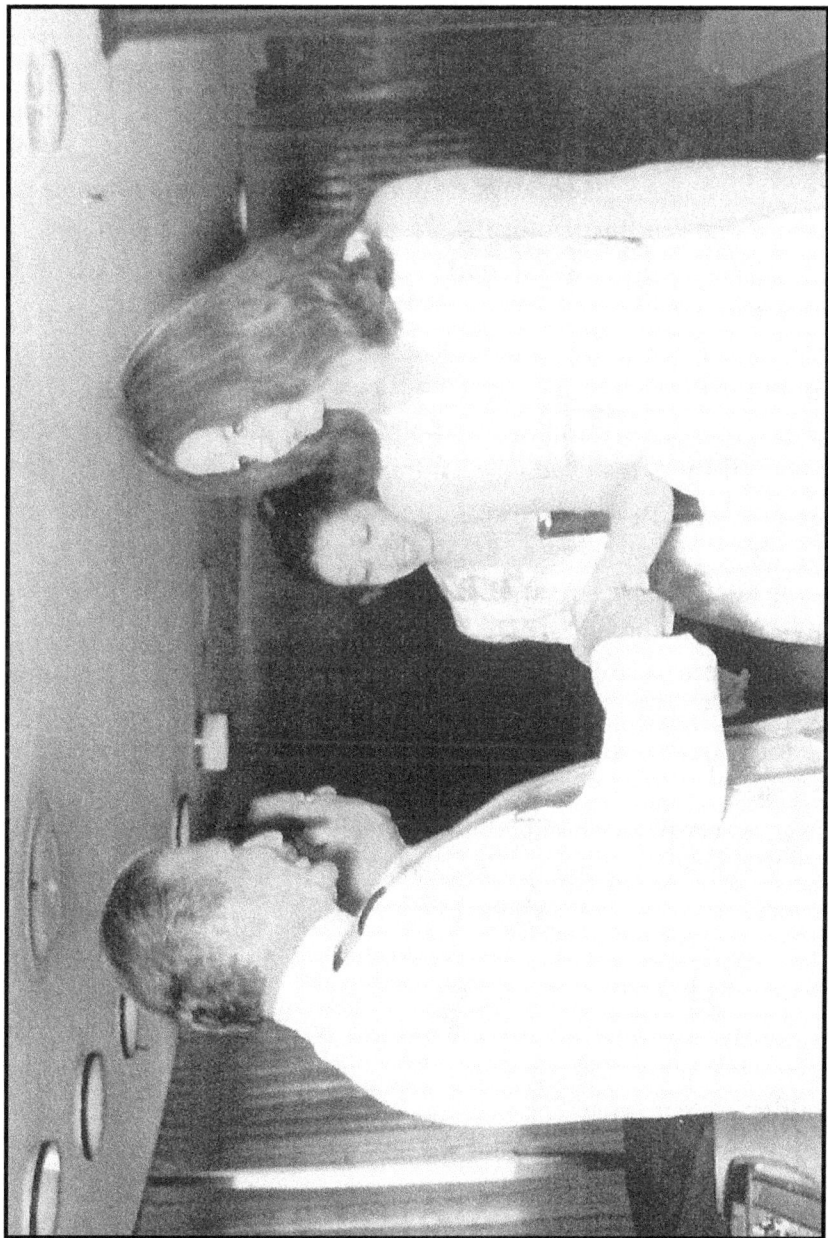

1972 Cruise

He was a well-dressed businessman, but he would never tell me anything about himself. I was sure he had given me a fake name. One night we were eating in a restaurant at a Hilton Hotel. I excused myself to go to the restroom, and instead went out front and copied his license number. A friend used the number to get the man's name for me. I never told him I knew his real name. He always treated me well but after a couple of years, he stopped calling. Ironically, a few years later I placed a personal ad (stating that I was a transsexual) in a local paper (Creative Loafing); he responded using his real name. I called the number he provided just to be sure it was the same person. When I recognized his voice, I hung up. I never heard from him again.

During the Christmas season of 1971, I attended one social event after another. I was involved with church and a Bible study group, and there were a lot of parties. This group with which I was involved knew nothing about my surgery and I had several dates within the group—including a date for New Year's Eve. I attended a party at the American Legion hall and had the best New Year's Eve of my life.

In the summer of 1972, a cousin and I took a cruise on the New Bahama Star. We must have had the smallest cabin on the ship. There was so little room that, if we were both out of bed at the same time, one of us had to be in the bathroom. We were disgusted—until we went to dinner.

We were very popular and invited to go out after dinner. I was invited out by five men and I stupidly agreed to go out with each of them. It was a small cruise ship—only two decks—and if I went out with one man, there was an excellent chance I might run into the others. I couldn't take that chance, so I had to spend my evening in the tiny cabin.

All but one of the men were members of the crew. The one who wasn't a crew member asked me out the next evening. One of the others was waiting for me when the ship docked at the end of the cruise. He, my cousin, her friend and I spent the day partying in Miami, and had an enjoyable day.

I had been introduced to the Georgia Public Health Information Officer, but I didn't really know him. One day he walked out of my boss's office, stopped and propped his foot on my desk to tie his shoe. While doing so, he asked if I would like to go for cocktails after work at Underground Atlanta. Naturally, I said yes. Underground was only a couple of blocks from the office so we walked. After a few drinks, he told me he didn't have a car and I would have to ride the bus home. I was enjoying being with him but that information was very sobering. I was ready to go when I learned I had to ride the bus home.

By the autumn of 1973, things began closing in on me. Every way I turned, I was bumping into people who knew a relative or someone with whom I had worked at Rich's. My best friend Ruth, told me that her husband and his sister had attended the same school I did. One day, she told me she had looked for my picture in a school yearbook.

During this time, I was having beard removed at an electrolysis school. Students came there from all over the country. One evening, the girl who was working on me asked me where I worked. When I told her, she mentioned one of the auditors in my office, and told me he was her best friend's husband. When she asked me if I knew him, I lied and said I didn't.

Another day, I went to the snack bar at work, and on my way out someone yelled out, "Phoebe!" I looked and saw someone who seemed very surprised to see me, someone I didn't recognize. I hurried out without saying a word.

Still another day, I ran into someone in the hall at work who was a friend of my cousin—the same cousin who had invited me out for that disastrous evening with her ex-husband and his friend, Mel. This man delighted in telling people about me at parties and clubs. He had gotten a temporary job with the state.

I tried to sound tough when I told him to keep his mouth shut about me. He replied, "I don't know anything about you, do I?"

I never saw him again at work, but one evening when I was out at a club; he said, in front of several people, "I keep wanting to call you J. C."

I told him, "You don't know me well enough to want to call me anything," which was true.

People I knew who knew my story shared it with people *they* knew—people who didn't know me and couldn't care less about me. This was becoming a major problem for me.

In the spring of 1974, things got worse. I had a surprise encounter with a pre-op transsexual I had spoken with by phone during the period I'd been assisting the organization that advocated for transsexuals. This individual had an appointment with an administrative assistant in Medicaid to see if they would pay for sex-change surgery.

Unbeknownst to me the Chief of Medicaid, Jack Moore knew about my surgery (his secretary was my best friend Ruth). Knowing that I suspected that my coworkers knew about my surgery, and knowing it would be upsetting to me if my suspicions were confirmed, he arranged for the interview to be moved to another office. The administrative assistant normally sat at a desk next to mine. The chief was trying to protect me from having contact with the pre-op transsexual. He didn't want the subject of transsexualism coming up in my presence.

Little did he know that this person would stop at my office door to ask for directions. When she did, I had no idea who she was or why she was there. When it was time to go home, I walked to the elevator with friends. When we got to the elevator, there she stood.

Someone mentioned my name and the pre-op woman said, "Excuse me, are you Miss Phoebe Smith?"

When I told her I was, she told me her name, which I recognized immediately. That did it—I nearly quit my job.

I was aware that people were now laughing and pointing at me when my friends and I went into the cafeteria. I suspected what was going on, but I couldn't be sure. I was a bundle of nerves.

Ruth had tried to talk with me about it once and although I suspected she knew, I could never bring myself to open up about it. One day after work, we were in the restroom and I told her that I felt she knew something she wasn't telling me. She stammered a little bit and said, "Phoebe, if it's your past you are worried about, we all know and we still love you."

I couldn't stop crying. She had known since October of the previous year, and so had quite a few others. Someone had distributed copies of a newspaper article about me. The article had been written about me having the surgery, and was done in the hopes of helping me find employment. Someone did promise me a job in their family grocery store but never came through with the job.

The conversation with Ruth occurred on Friday, and I told her I wouldn't be back to work. When she heard this, she told me I had a lot of friends, many of whom knew and were behind me one hundred percent.

When I was composed enough, she and her husband drove me home. I didn't want my parents to know what was going on. I had already caused them enough heartache. I figured I could have some privacy in the bathroom, so I immediately got into the bathtub, where I sat and cried. Ruth later told me she was very concerned that I might commit suicide that weekend. She was right to worry—it was very much on my mind.

Jack Moore became one of my best friends. He, Ruth and I had breakfast every morning in the state offices cafeteria. Occasionally he took us out to lunch, once to the Playboy Club. I left Medicaid in 1975 but we remained good friends. He and I often met for drinks after work. In the early eighties, we took a ten-week bartending class together. We would meet for dinner first and then go to class. We had practice bartending parties and each member of the class could invite two guests. We had a great time. We became certified bartenders but neither of us ever tended bar.

In his last years we stayed in touch but I rarely saw him. I felt a tremendous loss when he died as the result of a stroke he had suffered months earlier. I have never had another friend quite like him. I have missed him.

1974

TEN

The next week was hell. I knew most of the people in the building, and every time I saw someone, I wondered, *Do they know? And if they don't, how will they react when they find out?*

In addition to my regular job, I had a salaried part-time position with the Georgia Public Health Association (GPHA). I was associated with many of the members when I worked in the Health Department. It was a responsible position, and I couldn't just quit.

The following week was the annual meeting for GPHA, and I had to attend. I saw people constantly pointing me out. I'd had a lunch date with one of the exhibitors. We had a date for the evening as well, but he never showed up. I later saw him with one of the girls who was spreading my story. I didn't hate him—I hated her. In spite of it all, I had a fairly good time. The next evening I had a date with a very good looking man, and I made sure we were seen.

After a few weeks, I was more relaxed than I had been in a long time. A great burden had been lifted. After my story became common knowledge at work, I noticed that most of the men who had been quite friendly previously were now distant. One of my friends told me that someone had brought a copy of the newspaper article to work, and told her, "I thought you ought to know." Another told her, "I discussed Phoebe with my husband, and asked him how I should act toward her, and he told me to act the way I always act."

During my four years in Medicaid, leadership changed three or four times. One of the directors (Al) had been a federal employee. He often attended Medicaid meetings. He always stopped by my desk to chat (more like flirting). When he became director, he took the office occupied by my former boss. I was seated just outside his door, but I was not his secretary. When he needed someone to run an important errand, he often called on me.

Even though I didn't know shorthand, one of the duties of my job was to take minutes for the Medicaid Advisory Committee meetings. My friend, Ruth was an expert in shorthand and she rescued me.

During Al's time as director, we were gathered in a board room for an Advisory meeting. Ruth and I were at one end of the table; Al, board members and guests were at the other end. The room was full of people but the meeting was never called to order. There was a lot of whispering and after a while we were dismissed. I later learned that the whispering was about me. A doctor who had joined the Medicaid staff in an advisory position knew about my surgery and chose that time to inform Al.

After that meeting, Al never asked me to do anything for him again. He would speak to me in the mornings but he would not look at me. He wasn't in that position very long. I wasn't sorry to see him go.

The summer of 1974, I attended a nursing home convention at Jekyll Island, Georgia. I worked in the nursing home unit of Medicaid so I knew a lot of the owners and managers who were attending.

I was traveling with a coworker and a friend. We arrived a couple of days before the convention started. The first night we were there, we met some of the people we knew. One of the nursing home owners and I hit it off. We split away from the others and walked on the beach late in the night. I knew nothing about him personally except that I liked him. We spent time together the next evening and the next afternoon. The third night was the convention banquet. He invited me to go. We sat at the association president's table. At one point he brought his son to join us. He gave his son his chair and sat with me. I was surprised he had a son and I assumed he must be divorced. Otherwise, he surely would not have me sit at the president's table and certainly not with his son. I knew most of the people at the table and they were all friendly. I am sure they all thought I knew he was married, but I had no reason to suspect that he was. We had a great time. The next morning we went home.

The next week he was in Atlanta and I went out with him and asked him about his family and he told me he was married. During the conversation I asked him if he knew my situation. He said he had heard something about it but didn't know if it was true. I saw him a couple of times at the office after that. We acted as if we had never had an encounter.

One night, I was dancing on a crowded floor with a man who didn't know about my surgery. All of a sudden, I became aware that everyone around us had stopped dancing. Looking around, it didn't take long for me to discover the reason. A girl who worked across the hall from me had told those around her, and it spread around the dance floor.

In 1975 I changed positions at work, transferring from Medicaid to Family and Children Services. At the time, I didn't know if any of my new coworkers knew about my surgery. I worked in the Policies and Procedures Unit, which included a unit chief, three policy writers (Ann, Susan, and Robertia), and two secretaries other than myself. One day I was in Ann's office when Susan rushed in, closed the door, and exclaimed, "Y'all, there is a transsexual that works for the state!"

I was so stunned, I left the room. I went to my best friend Ruth and told her what had happened.

After I left the office, Ann said, "Susan, it's Phoebe." Apparently Susan and our unit chief were about the only ones that didn't know. I learned that day that the Division Director and most of the others knew.

Around this same time, a female coworker of mine attended a funeral, and happened to sit by a distant relative of mine who told her, "Phoebe used to be a man."

For the most part, I was blessed to have coworkers who were understanding, and to some extent, protective of me. But every day it was something. The office was being painted and one of the painters was about to paint above my desk. I asked him if he wanted me to move. When he responded, he called me, "Sir." He turned out to be the nephew of a distant relative.

Still another time, a cashier in the cafeteria turned to a coworker, pointed at me and said, "that's the one I was telling you about"!

In 1975, I skipped the GPHA convention. In 1976, I went—and regretted it. At a party in the president-elect's room, a young man I didn't know walked up to me and asked me if I was a man. I later learned that someone had told him to do it.

I was very upset and went to my room. I was hurt that even a stranger would do such a thing. I went again the next year. My main reason for going was to let them all see that I would not be beaten. That year, there were no incidents. By then, my role had increased considerably. Initially, I'd been in charge of pre-registration. My duties increased to include membership and registration at the convention.

One day in late 1976, I received a call from the employment counselor who had tried to help me find a job a few years earlier. He wanted me to stop by his office, which was just a couple of blocks away.

A few days later I did stop by to see him. His secretary announced me and I went into his office. He closed the door, swung me around and kissed me. I was floored. All the while we were talking, he never let go of my hand. During the conversation, he suggested we get a room, but I was not interested.

A few years later, he stopped by my office and again suggested we get a room. He said I would have to get the room because he was so well known. He obviously thought I was desperate. I never saw him again but he called from time to time.

In early 1979, a friend and I went out for drinks. When we got in the car to leave, the car wouldn't start. I never learned to drive, and knew nothing about cars. She didn't know what to do either. A man parked next to us was getting out of his car and saw that we were having trouble and came over to help. He got the car started for us. I was sitting in the passenger seat, but caught a glimpse of him while my friend was thanking him. I wanted to meet him, so I suggested we buy him a drink to thank him for his assistance.

He accepted the invitation, and we spent a couple of hours with him. He invited me out the following evening—a Friday. When we went out that evening, he told me that he was from New Jersey, and explained that he went home on Friday evenings and returned on Sunday evenings. After our date, he headed home to New Jersey.

He called me on Saturday from New Jersey and invited me to dinner the next evening. We went out two to three times a week, and on Wednesday afternoons, he rented a small plane so we could fly over Atlanta and the surrounding areas. He always went home Friday evenings, called me on Saturdays and was back on Sunday evening.

When I told him about my surgery, he said, "Miss Smith, you are something else!"

I should have known it was too good to be true. In early May, he told me he was going to be transferred to another location. I was devastated. He even told me the location. The next week, I wanted to talk with him, so I called the number for the location he had given me. They had never heard of him. I then called the hotel where he always stayed while in Atlanta, and asked for his room.

When he answered, I was stunned. I held the phone briefly, and hung up. He called me immediately and said he was coming to pick me up. Dumb me, I still hadn't figured it out.

We went back to his room to talk, and he told me he knew it was me that had called. He told me that the transfer had been delayed a couple of weeks, and he thought it best to leave things the way they were. I believed him and I continued to see him.

Around the first of June, he said he had to take some time off work to take care of some things in New Jersey before the transfer, and would call me when he returned. After a few days, I started to wonder why he couldn't call like he usually did when he went to New Jersey. He had given me the name of the city where he lived in New Jersey, so I called information for that city, and asked the operator if she had a listing for him.

She replied, "No, but we have a listing for that name in another city." She gave me the number and when I called, a woman answered. I asked if I had reached his residence, and she replied, "Yes, I'm his wife."

I was so upset, I couldn't go to work the next day. The following Sunday, he called and said "I'm back." We didn't go out that night but the next night, we went to dinner. After we had been there a few minutes, I asked him, "Are you married?"

He said, "No! Why would you ask me that?"

Then I told him what I had done.

He said, "Okay, I'm married but we are not happy."

When I asked him if they were getting a divorce, he said, "No, she's the one who has the money." He explained that his job had initially been temporary but had become permanent, so his wife and daughter were moving here also.

I was so hooked on him, I continued to see him until she moved here, and a couple times afterwards as well. Finally, he said he had to stop seeing me because his wife had become suspicious; that was probably a lie. It took me two years to get over that situation.

ELEVEN

In June of 1979, I self-published a small book entitled *Phoebe*. At the time I published it, I had no idea who knew my story and who didn't. Therefore, I had to assume that everyone knew. That assumption caused me to appear unfriendly and cautious—a demeanor that discouraged people from wanting to get to know me.

So, why did I act that way? Ten years of experience had taught me that it was far better – easier perhaps – for me to be aloof, to appear non-caring though I did care. To protect myself, I didn't get easily involved so when someone discovered my secret, I was less vulnerable. When I was with people I didn't know, it proved to be less painful for me to be on guard at all times and that was costly.

Certain situations were more difficult to navigate than others. For example, it was especially challenging when I found myself in a group of people that included some who knew and some who didn't. Some people would never tell, while others were delighted to tell and then watch me to see how I would handle it.

If a man in a group where some of the people knew and others did not seemed interested in me, I had to be very cautious. There was no way to know how a person would react to being told about my surgery. Sometimes a man who had been friendly before he learned of my surgery would completely ignore me after he was informed.

Once my book was published, I got mixed reactions at work. People I hadn't known previously became friendly. No man from work ever asked me out again. When all was said and done, the book accomplished one very important thing—there was no more obvious laughing and pointing at me in the workplace. I sent the TV news person that I had met in 1971, a flyer about my book. I never heard from him again; that was certainly understandable.

In 1980, I put together a brochure entitled, "The Journey from One to Forty was Difficult but Successful". It included the photo of me and my father made on my first birthday and a photo of me at age forty. It read as follows:

Several months ago, a doctor involved with a study concerning the success of transsexuals at the Johns Hopkins Gender Identity Clinic released statements for a newspaper article. This study involved fifty gender disoriented individuals. Fifteen had change-of-sex surgery; thirty-five underwent psychiatric counseling. This study determined that there was no real difference in later adjustment between those who had the surgery and those who underwent psychiatric counseling.

The Johns Hopkins Clinic enforces strict guidelines. To say that fifteen out of fifteen post-op transsexuals failed to adjust is, in my opinion, an admission that those in the professional roles made errors in judgment at some point. (Maybe they chose the wrong fifteen for surgery.)

The success of each individual's adjustment could only be compared to his or her previous existence, not another transsexual and certainly no one else.

A uniform diagnosis could only be the result of conformity. I can't believe this study netted a group of conformers. Transsexuals do not conform as readily as those who are not. If one is strong enough to face society after having sex-change surgery, he or she surely is strong enough to be an

individual. Therein lies the problem. Society accepts con-
formers not individuals. A society conforming to wear the
blanket of "normalcy" can be strong; it can also be cruel
to one who doesn't choose to wear the blanket. (Being nor-
mal does not mean being like everyone else; being normal
means being individual—unlike everyone else.)...

At thirty years [old] with less than a high school education
and no record of any kind to document my existence, I had
to cover my past to get a job. I have worked for the State
of Georgia for almost ten years. During my fourth year
of employment, knowledge of my surgery became wide-
spread. It was upsetting, but also a big relief to get it in the
open. Luckily, I have an understanding family and I had
friends who assured me of their support.

Today, eleven years after surgery, I am a busy and happy
woman. In addition to my secretarial job with the state, I
have a telephone wakeup service and every other Saturday,
I work for a large law firm assembling wills on a word pro-
cessor. Two years ago, I bought a duplex as an investment. I
am also rather social. (I am reasonably attractive and I have
dated quite a few men who never knew I was once a male.)

Last year, I published the story of my life in a paperback
book. I wrote it, typed it, and handled all the details with
no representation and no promotion except a flyer I pre-
pared. Most of the books have been sold.

I do not present myself as a transsexual role model; however,
I do consider myself a successful person. I do not believe the
fact that I had sex-change surgery is a determining factor.
Others, I am sure, have been more successful. I have made
mistakes; being an achiever, I am willing to make more.

I do not know another (post-op) transsexual. The only one I ever met was in the hospital for surgery at the same time I was. I have talked with numerous transsexuals via phone and corresponded with far more from all over the United States who were contemplating sex-change surgery. From this experience, I know transsexuals come in all races, rich, poor, both sexes, all sizes; and the desire for sex-change surgery does not subside after a certain age. One of my correspondents had sex-change surgery at the age of fifty-eight.

I also believe that the best research can never produce a cure for transsexualism or sidetrack a transsexual. My basis for this is the belief that there could never be a proper time to apply the antidote. If the situation is recognizable, there is no remedy. One who can be dissuaded never was a transsexual in the total sense of the word.

Society as a whole has no desire for us to succeed and when a professional (especially one with the clout of John Hopkins) makes documented statements, realistic or not, in the eyes of society, that's the way it is. BUT THAT IS NOT THE WAY IT IS!

As a transsexual who is 'making it,' I have an obligation to myself and to anyone else who might benefit to do whatever I can to improve the situation. Why me? Why not me?

To remain silent is to accept— to accept is to agree. I do not agree with, nor do I accept society's placement of me or anyone else who is unfortunate enough to require sex-change surgery. I have no doubt that the day will come when the word transsexual will no longer be a brow-raising word. However, it will not happen without the battle.

TWELVE

My social life was now comprised primarily of occasional dates and going out dancing with friends and cousins. Whenever I was in a public place, I always scanned the environment to see if there was anyone there who knew me. Sometimes there was, and sometimes I was recognized by people I didn't know.

I wanted a more active social life, so I placed an ad in a local personal column. The ad led to a few dates, but I wasn't comfortable having the ad run again in an Atlanta paper. So, I placed a personal ad in *the Village Voice* in New York. I subscribed to *the Village Voice* for years. There was information in its pages that I couldn't find anywhere else.

My ad began with the phrase, "Sue Ellen lookalike." The TV show "Dallas" was very popular at the time, and so was one of the lead characters on the show, Sue Ellen. I had been told that I looked like her by several strangers—a waitress, a patient in a doctor's office, and others. I didn't see the resemblance, but obviously others did. My ad also stated, "There's a story on me." When I received a response from someone, I told them the story.

I ran the ad twice in *the Village Voice,* and received many replies from some very nice people. I didn't say there were Sunday school teachers - not all Sunday school teachers are nice. I now had a very busy social life, but not one that I could really talk about. Of course, they all knew about my surgery, which was part of the attraction. Some were impressed that I had the guts to place the ad.

One of the men was an actor in a soap opera; I also saw him in a Elvis movie. Most of them were businessmen. Some of them I saw only once. Although I had never heard of him, one of the men was well known. He didn't like to go to the popular night spots, but that was fine with me, I enjoyed his company. I saw him quite a few times, the last time being in 1991. That was the last date I ever had with anyone.

Such as it was, it was the best social period of my life. During that period of dating, the only gift I ever accepted was a round-trip airline ticket and a bottle of Johnny Walker Black scotch. I had hoped I would end up in a permanent relationship as a result of this ad, but that wasn't to be.

Because of my surgery, I was a guest on a call-in radio program for several weeks. The time slot was midnight until 4:00 a.m. There were calls from all types of people—curious people, nice people, and nasty people. The nastiest were the religious people, especially a minister.

In September of 1980, due to a mass reorganization, a new communications office was established at the State Division of Family and Children's Services, and I was given a new position as its supervisor. The director of the section that included my unit downgraded my pay by two pay grades—but not my title or workload. This was done before my new position even became effective. My supervisor tried to prevent this from happening but the section director wouldn't change his mind. I never thought his decision had anything to do with my surgery.

My job was very responsible. All printed communications for mass distribution from the State DFCS' offices to county departments passed through the communications office. I liked the job, and stayed with it until late 1983 when I got a job in a different unit in DFACS. (I remained on that job until I retired on October 31, 2000.)

My boss, prior to the re-organization was a member of an organization called The Friendship Force, and she encouraged me to join.

Friendship Force International is a nonprofit exchange organization promoting friendship and goodwill through a program of homestay exchanges. It was founded in Atlanta, Georgia in 1977 by President Jimmy Carter. In April of 1981, I went with a group of Friendship Force members on a ten-day trip to Cali, Colombia as part of the exchange program.

I spoke no Spanish, and stayed with a young Colombian family who spoke no English. We smiled a lot. In exchange, this family had a family member stay in the home of someone in the U.S. Typically it would have been my home in which the family member stayed, but there were more homes available in Atlanta than were needed.

They lived in a modern subdivision in a nice house, but the mattress on my bed was stuffed with hay! I wondered if I'd made a mistake in coming. Some of the people with older homes parked their cars in their living room at night because of crime. One of the living room walls had a built-in garage door.

A friend of my hosts had lived in the States for several years, so he stayed the first night to serve as interpreter. Before I went to bed, I locked my door. Then, I decided I'd better unlock it. It occurred to me that, if my hosts discovered it locked, they might think I didn't trust them. I didn't want to give them that impression, so I unlocked it.

I should have left it locked. Sometime during the night, I was awakened by the interpreter getting into bed with me. At my insistence, he left. The following day (Sunday) he acted as if the incident had never happened, and I did too.

We spent the day visiting my hosts' friends and family. I enjoyed the day, and was glad to be there. That first day, we visited a restaurant, and when I went to the restroom I was shocked at what I found. There was no commode, only a slanted floor with water running through to carry out the waste.

That night, we attended a meeting, along with other guests and their hosts. Friendship Force officials advised us of things we should and should not do. One thing we were cautioned against was traveling in areas not designated or approved for us. In other words, they wanted us to advise them if we planned to travel outside the designated areas. There were areas of unrest in Colombia.

On Monday morning, my hosts' English-speaking friend told me that he and his family were going on Easter vacation to Ecuador. I told him I would miss him. That was my first mistake.

He replied, "Well, would you like to go?" I agreed to join him—and that was my second mistake.

They planned to leave the following morning, so we had to get busy to put things in order. I called the number I had for the trip coordinator for the Friendship Force. The person I spoke with couldn't answer my questions as to what I might need for my trip to Ecuador.

So, my hosts' friend contacted a Colombian official to find out what kind of pass or permit I would need to travel from Colombia to Ecuador, and back. He was told that all we needed was a vehicular pass, indicating the number of people traveling in the vehicle. That sounded simple enough—in fact, way too simple. If all the passengers had been Colombian, there would have been no problem.

Tuesday morning before dawn ten of us departed Cali in a pickup truck. We drove all day and the first night, stopping only for food and bathroom breaks. Finally we arrived at the border, where we saw a line of people. They were entering a trailer on the Colombia side and exiting on the Ecuador side.

When I reached the desk inside, I showed my ID and the exit card I would need when I left Colombia to return home to the States. The clerk took my exit card, refused to return it to me, and motioned for me to keep moving. Before I knew what was happening, I was in Ecuador. It happened so fast, I was stunned. The man who had invited me to come along told me not to worry about it.

The next night, we drove into the lobby of a hotel, checked in, and spent the night. It may sound funny to say we drove into the lobby of a hotel, but this wasn't like the lobby of a Hilton. The drive into the hotel was between two buildings in the middle of a block. It was more like a covered barn, with parking on one side and registration on the other. There were two floors with rooms, with staircases leading up to them.

The following morning, we had breakfast in the hotel restaurant. I ordered coffee with cream, and received a cup of hot milk with a jar of instant coffee. Later that day, we did some sightseeing and visited the Equator.

The next day, we headed back to Cali, sightseeing along the way. We saw many beautiful churches, and stopped at every one of them. The family with whom I was traveling was very religious.

Apparently, Easter is family vacation time in that region because hotel rooms were scarce. The last night of the trip, all ten of us slept in the same room—and we had to pass through someone else's room to access ours. We awakened the people in the other room as we passed through, and they were very annoyed with us.

I needed to go to the bathroom but there wasn't one in sight. I was afraid to go looking for one by myself. Thank God for Imodium. By the following morning, we all had to go. There was only one bathroom, and it was on the roof! There was a long line for the bathroom, and it only accommodated one person at a time.

By the time we left Ecuador, I was more than ready to get back to my hosts' house in Cali. I was still shaving at that time, and somewhere along the way, I had lost my razor. Now, the hair on my neck was becoming noticeable. I told my friend I needed to buy a razor so I could shave my legs.

It was late afternoon when we reached the Colombian border. I was nervous because my exit pass had been confiscated as I'd entered Ecuador. My friend assured me that there would be no problem, and I tried to remain calm.

No one had a problem but me. The guards would not allow me to cross the border without identification. I was terrified. Neither my family nor anyone else was aware that I was in Ecuador. I was crying, praying and wishing I had never left home.

My friend promised me that we would drive until we could find a place to cross the border where there were no guards. Thankfully, we did so without incident. I was still scared when we arrived back in Cali late Sunday evening, because I was now illegally in Colombia.

The first thing I did after we arrived back in Cali was to call the tour coordinator. I started crying, and explained, "You are not going to believe what I did…" I was afraid he was going to fuss at me, but he told me to calm down and assured me that everything was going to be okay. He instructed me to go to the American Consulate or Embassy, and told me that they would help me.

On Monday morning, I visited both places. The first place I went told me to go to the other one. The man who helped me seemed to be very angry. He was waving his arms and yelling at my friend. I was afraid I was going to jail, but after a few minutes, he wrote something in my passport and stamped it. Then he said, in perfect English, "I hope you enjoyed your visit to Colombia."

On Monday night, I took my host family and some of my new friends to dinner to thank them for their hospitality. Some of them gave me gifts. On Tuesday, we visited the other people I had spent time with, so I could say goodbye. We left Colombia on Wednesday morning. Once we were finally in the air, I completely relaxed for the first time since the border incident.

As much as I enjoyed the trip, I was glad to be home again and back to my regular routine.

On a Swinging Bridge Near Cali Colombia - 1981

THIRTEEN

There were one thousand copies in the first printing of my book, *PHOEBE*. A New York bookstore bought four hundred copies, and I sold the remaining copies in person or by mail. The sale of these books generated quite a bit of mail from people seeking information. I became aware of the need for a reliable and easy to access source of information.

I communicated with the individuals who had purchased the book, asking if they would be interested in a newsletter. When I was sure there was sufficient interest, I began to working on the *first issue of THE TRANSASEXUAL VOICE. The first two issues were complimentary. I printed thirty copies of the first issue. Within a few months I had over one hundred subscribers.*

I never learned to drive and there were times when I had a problem getting the newsletters printed when I needed them. I needed to locate a printer convenient to where I lived. I found one located on Central Avenue in Hapeville within five miles of my house.

When I dropped an issue off to be printed, the woman who assisted was very personable. She told me my work would be ready in two days. The next day I received a call from her, informing me that they were swamped with work and could not print my work. Apparently she did not know what the content of my newsletter was about when she accepted it. After I picked it up, I asked a friend to call and ask if they could print something for her with the identical number of pages and same number of copies with a two-day turnaround. She was told it would be no problem.

Fortunately, I located a KWIK KOPY near my office and I used them until I discontinued the newsletter.

In 1982, a subscriber wanted to put an advertisement in the newsletter. He owned electrolysis equipment and was seeking someone to train who also needed electrolysis. In 1969 I paid twenty dollars per hour for electrolysis – that was a lot of money at that time – I jumped at the chance. After he trained me, I worked on him for an hour and he worked on me for an hour. We did this for at least fifteen years. It saved me tons of money and got rid of my unwanted hair. Along the way, I made a good friend.

By the mid-eighties, I had over three hundred subscribers from quite a few different countries. Many subscribers provided articles on a regular basis; more notably, Dr. Leo Wollman (an associate of Dr. Harry Benjamin), Sister Mary Elizabeth, Rupert Raj, Sandra Mesics and Michelle Hunt. Michelle was a nurse and had a regular column called THE NURSE'S STATION. She put together a package for transsexuals to have sex-change surgery in Brussels, Belguim. She made all the arrangements, accompanied the patient and was their nurse throughout the stay in Belguim. She provided a valuable service

Based on correspondence I received from subscribers I wrote the following article for *the Transsexual Voice.*

OPINIONS

Some of you have been with me from the beginning. Some of you were pre-op then and are now post-op. Some of you were pre-op then, are pre-op now, and will be pre-op until the day you die. For some, to be pre-op seems to be enough; that being the case, that is all they should ever be.

Are they really transsexuals? Pre means before...before what? If you don't have the SRS or at least plan to, how could you have ever been pre-op? Someone once told me, "I used to be a pre-op transsexual." I asked "What happened?" The answer was, "Oh, I stopped taking hormones."

Everyone who ever lived must have wondered at some time or another what it would be like to be the other sex (privately, of course). My point—if you are a transsexual, do it all the way. If you are not, stop fooling yourself. If you don't know, find out. Life is too short to waste.

I have received letters from a lot of people who say they should have had the surgery a long time ago but now feel it is too late. Others have it in their twilight years and say they have never been happier. And lastly, there are those who had the surgery and wish they hadn't.

Recently, I talked with someone who had the SRS a couple of years ago and whom I thought was very happy (she is successful). She told me that she was not happy she had gone through with it. I had talked with this person several times during the past five years. During this time, she ran hot and cold; part of the time she was sure she wasn't going to have the surgery; other times she was sure she was going to have it. She now has regrets and still has sessions with her psychiatrist.

If you have doubts, remove them; they won't go away by themselves. If you are afraid, then you are going to find lots of reasons to be afraid because you are looking for them. If you are not afraid, you won't be looking for reasons to be afraid. If you act ashamed, then people will treat you as if you should be ashamed. If you show them you have no reason to be ashamed, you will be treated accordingly.

Life is a gift. The instructions are a little bit difficult to follow sometimes but just remember, GOD CREATED US ALL EQUALLY DIFFERENT. He planned us all the way and he has no favorites. You owe it to yourself to be happy. If SRS is what it takes for you to be happy…it's up to you. I know how easy it is to want something, to be afraid of it and all that it can evoke. I was there once. I assure you, I have never regretted even once that I had the SRS.

✢ ✢ ✢

Throughout the eighties, I mailed packets of transsexual-related material to newspaper editors, TV news programs, and talk show hosts and anyone else that I thought might read it. One day I mailed thirty-two packets to various people. I received a reply from Dennis Wholey, the host of the 'America's Live Call-in Talk Show' No one else responded. One of the others was the host of occasional nighttime TV specials. I never heard from him but one night I was watching his show and he repeated the following just as I had written it: "We are dealing with the more advanced society that once burned-at-the-stake those suspected of practicing witchcraft and more recently were inhumane to the mentally ill and epileptics." That statement was included in an article I wrote for THE TRANSSEXUAL VOICE and was included in the packet I sent to him

1983

1985

1992

1993

FOURTEEN

September of 1983 was the beginning of a long and difficult period for my family. My mother had pneumonia, and spent several days in the hospital.

In November, my father had prostate surgery. After the surgeon finished, and while my father was still sedated, his lung doctor wanted to check his lungs. In doing so, he punctured a lung. My father was on life support for eight days and in ICU for a several more days. He was moved to a private room, but couldn't speak because of the tube that had been down his throat.

One day while my aunt was visiting my father in the hospital, an orderly got him up to go to the bathroom, and dropped him on the commode. My father couldn't talk, and my aunt did not know the fall had injured him. He was in the hospital for sixty days. After he returned home, he couldn't walk, and had constant back pain. He now had only twenty-five percent of his lung capacity and was on oxygen, but he was still smoking.

After a month, my father was readmitted to the hospital, and found to have fractured vertebrae. We decided to sue the hospital, and obtained an attorney. He said we had a good case, and he began working on it right away.

My brother Billy was diagnosed with cancer in early August of 1984. It was in his brain and lung. We were heartbroken. I felt helpless in trying to comfort my parents.

I had planned to attend a lifestyles convention in Las Vegas in August as an exhibitor, but in light of my brother's health, I was hesitant to go. I decided that I should keep my plans.

My father developed skin cancer on one ear, and it progressed to the stage that he required radiation. He and my brother went together for radiation treatments. My father's treatment was successful.

On Thanksgiving Day of that year, Billy had the first of several seizures. He died four months later at the age of forty. We were devastated by my brother's death. I was five years older than he was; I thought I would always have him.

Within five weeks of my brother's death, we lost my aunt—the one who witnessed the orderly dropping my father. The attorney who had been handling daddy's case against the hospital told my father that without my aunt's testimony, he had no case.

My father wasn't able to do yard work anymore, so I took it over. I wore three inch heels when I cut grass because the only flats I had was a pair of flip flops. Eventually, I took over the cooking too, despite the fact that I knew very little about cooking. Both my parents were in very poor health, and the doctor bills and prescriptions were a constant financial drain. There was no money to hire outside help.

In December of 1988, my parents celebrated their fiftieth wedding anniversary.

On May 30th, 1989, my mother had a cervical fusion. My father could hardly walk, but he drove to the hospital to see her. In early July, he fell and broke his hip and spent some time in the hospital. When they were both back home, I hired someone to stay with them for four hours each day, from 10 a.m. until 2 p.m.

I was getting very little sleep and was exhausted, but I had to work. One day I went out to lunch with coworkers and on the way to the restaurant, I had an anxiety attack. I couldn't stop crying. I took two days off work to recover from all the stress.

My father died on August 7th, 1989, three days after his seventy-fourth birthday.

Mother's health continued to deteriorate but she was able to stay by herself in the daytime while I worked until 1993. For the next four and a half years, I hired my cousin Melba to stay with her during the day while I worked.

In 1995, I had to discontinue the newsletter I had been publishing for fourteen years because of the level of care my mother required. It was hard to abandon the newsletter. I had created it from nothing and it meant a lot to me.

In 1995, a new position was created in my office. It came with a higher pay grade than my job, so I applied for it. I had the highest score on the State Merit System Register for that position. Since I was already in the Section, I felt pretty good about getting the job. Quite a few applications were received, but no interviews were conducted.

I was stunned when I heard that the job was being advertised again. This meant that I wasn't being considered. I got to work before most of my coworkers, so I went into the office where the applications were kept and removed mine. When I told my supervisor and his supervisor what I had done, they both insisted that I return my application to the folder.

They said, "There is no way they cannot give you that job with your score!"

So I put my application back—but interviews were conducted, and I didn't get the job.

Something one of my coworkers shared with me shed light on the situation. My coworker's supervisor had told her that, when he'd told the Section director that another coworker was gay, the section director told the supervisor to fire the gay employee.

I asked my coworker if she would put that statement in writing and sign it.

She said, "Hell, no! And if you tell anyone, I'll just say, 'That bitch is lying!'"

Considering my Merit System Score, the fact that I was already in the section, and the fact that I now had my coworker's verbal statement of the incident, I felt I had grounds to file a complaint. So, I contacted a lawyer, who asked me to make an appointment to see him.

After a lot of questions and answers, the attorney told me that he didn't think any attorney in Atlanta would take a case like mine against the State of Georgia. When I asked him why he'd asked me to come in, he said, "I wanted to see what you looked like." At least he was honest.

I went to the personnel office at work to find out what I needed to do to file a federal discrimination complaint.

After a few months, the Section Director and Unit Chief got even with me for filing a complaint. They put me under a different supervisor, and made him do their dirty work. It wasn't long before the new supervisor called me into his office, and told me that he had some good news and some bad news. They would raise my job title to the same title as the job I had applied for—but I would receive no salary increase.

I tried to decline, but it was a done deal. I didn't have the option of refusing it.

My former supervisor had retired. I had already been assigned most of his job duties. They became my duties in addition to my own job duties and the duties connected with the new job title. The new job duties required training, and there was not enough time to do all I was given to do. My new supervisor and I constantly butted heads.

One day, I got a call from a lady with the U.S. Equal Employment Opportunity Commission. I told her that I was completely disgusted with the whole situation and everyone involved, and all I wanted to do was put it behind me. I explained that I was dropping the complaint.

She had a very sweet disposition, and during our conversation, she asked how long it would be until I could retire. When I told her, she started giving me reasons why I should not continue with the complaint. I had already told her I wanted to drop it.

Later, I received the following letter indicating a ruling was made against me. (I am referred to in the letter as the Charging Party.) It was also sent to the Georgia Department of Human Resources:

> *On behalf of the Commission, I issue the following deter-mination on the merits of the subject charge. All require-ments for coverage have been met. Substantial weight has been accorded to the findings of the Commission on Equal Opportunity, and having examined that agency's find-ings and the record presented, I conclude that evidence obtained during the investigation did not establish viola-tions of Federal statutes under the jurisdiction of EEOC.*
>
> *This determination and dismissal concludes the process-ing of this charge. This letter will be the only notice of dis-missal and the only notice of the Charging Party's right to sue sent by the Commission. Following this dismissal, the Charging Party may only pursue this matter by filing suit against the respondent named in the charge within 90 days of receipt of this letter. Otherwise, the Charging Party's right to sue will be lost.*
>
> *You are reminded that Federal law prohibits retaliation against persons who have exercised their right to inquire or complain about matters they believe may violate the law. Discrimination against persons who have cooperated in Commission investigations is also prohibited. This pro-tection applies regardless of the Commission's determina-tion on the merits of the charge.*
>
> *Bernice Williams-Kimbrough*
>
> *Acting District Director*

When I read this, I wanted to slap her. I thought I could count on someone in her position to do the right thing – like tell the truth. Apparently, I was wrong. Experience has taught me that very few people in positions of authority will do the right thing if they have a way out of it. I'm sure this woman was commended for a job well done.

I learned that the person who got the job I'd applied for had been heard bragging that the section director was his brother's neighbor. That explained everything. After a few months, he was transferred to another section and was soon fired.

A few months later, I was very surprised when my supervisor called me in, and asked me if I wanted my old job title back. That would entail my previous duties as well as the duties of my former supervisor who had retired. I was glad to make the switch.

I never knew why the section director was brought to the state offices from his job in South Georgia, but everyone knew high-ranking county employees were sometimes brought to the state offices when they screwed up in the county; I don't think that was true in his situation. It was said that the Unit Chief was brought in because of a complaint filed against him in the county where he worked. He was brought to the state DFCS office where he became unit chief, and later, section director. By the way – I liked him; I did not like the section director.

FIFTEEN

One morning when I was getting ready to go to work, I noticed that my mother was slurring her words and having trouble standing up. I thought she'd had a stroke so I called for an ambulance to take her to the hospital's emergency room. Her neurologist happened to be in the hospital at the time and was summoned to the ER. He agreed that she might have had a stroke, and told me he'd like to admit her for a twenty-three hour stay for an MRI.

The following morning, a couple of hours after mother was taken for an MRI, a representative from the doctor's office came to my mother's hospital room. She had a nurse with her. They told me that mother had gone into respiratory failure during the procedure. I had heard the Code Blue but it never occurred to me that it had anything to do with my mother.

I was escorted to the Intensive Care Unit, and was shocked when I saw my mother. She was unconscious and had bruises on her chest and arms. She spent several days in the hospital, and during that time, they found no indication that she had suffered a stroke.

When she came home from the hospital, she was put back on the same fifteen medications—and the same symptoms occurred. I bought a Physician's Desk Reference and read about her meds. One of them was for seizures, but she didn't suffer from seizures. The warning on another medication stated that it could cause symptoms of a stroke. I took her off both medications and the stroke symptoms disappeared.

A few months later, she was back in the hospital. The doctor who admitted her was a partner of her neurologist. He couldn't come up with a diagnosis and in conversation with her was very rude to her in my presence. I called his office and told the receptionist that I did not want him to attend to my mother in the hospital.

The next day, another of the partners came in. He was very pleasant, and after talking with mother and me, called in her endocrinologist. The tests the endocrinologist ran at that time led him to tell me that my mother had symptoms of Cushing's Syndrome and Addison's Disease, and that it was not possible for her to have both. I already knew my mother had Cushing's. She had a fatty tumor on the back of her neck, which is a symptom of Cushing's. I asked the endocrinologist if it was possible that she might have had Cushing's first and then developed Addison's. He was bewildered.

It was determined that she should have another MRI. This time, I accompanied her to the MRI center. I told the technician what had happened during her first MRI. It turned out that this was the technician who had done mother's first MRI. She told me that they had left pillows under mother's head and it had cut off her air supply. (Mother was a heavy woman at that time.) When I told a cousin about the incident, she told me I had grounds for a lawsuit, but I was too tired to pursue it.

The endocrinologist told me that my mother was too complicated for him. I'm sure part of the problem was caused by too many doctors attending to her—a neurologist, endocrinologist, urologist, cardiologist, gastroenterologist, orthopedist and dentist.

Her neck had been fractured in the 1953 car wreck, and as I mentioned, in 1989 she had cervical fusion. Her neurologist told me that mother's neck was a mass of arthritis, and that she also had arthritis from head to toe.

The numerous medications she'd been taking for so long had caused infection in her gums. (After her hysterectomy in 1946, she should have been given estrogen. If she had been prescribed estrogen at that time, she would have had a very different life, but it was not used for that treatment in those days. She was prescribed an antidepressant in her mid-thirties and took it most of her life. She developed many of the possible side effects.)

Her dentist pulled an abscessed tooth and caused an opening to her sinus cavity. I didn't think a dentist would ever pull an abscessed tooth. After that, when she drank water, it came out her nose. An oral surgeon repaired that, but the infection in her gums caused her blood sugar to be extremely high. Even with the maximum number of pills and two shots per day, her sugar was still between four and five hundred and she passed out several times per day.

I took her to a different dentist and he determined that her gums were the cause for the infection (a result of all the medication she had been prescribed). He suggested that her teeth be pulled, but he was hesitant to do so because of all her health problems. He discussed it with her doctor at Emory and it was decided that it should be done in the hospital. At age 75, she had all her remaining teeth pulled. She was in the hospital for three days and by the time she came home, her blood sugar had returned to normal.

Mother had a stroke when she was seventy-six. When the doctor told me she'd had a deep stroke and it had only affected her speech, I didn't believe him. She was already bedridden and unconscious at that time, and I saw no obvious signs of a stroke. When she awoke, it was clear that the doctor had been right about the stroke. When she tried to speak, it was gibberish. After a few weeks, her speech became much better. On some days she talked fine, but on other days I still couldn't understand anything she said.

Mother was in the hospital three times in the fall of 1997. She died on February 28th, 1998 at the age of seventy-seven. I was fifty-nine years old and alone for the first time in my life.

In addition to missing her terribly, it was the first time in several years that I wasn't the caretaker for one or both of my parents. It's quite an adjustment to suddenly not be needed after having someone depending on you.

If I ever did anything good in my life, it was to take care of my parents when they became too ill to care for themselves. Fortunately, neither of them ever had to go to a nursing home. Prior to their deaths, they both would have been classified as skilled-nursing-home patients. Mother's doctor tried several times to get me to put her in a nursing home, but I refused. He said she would be eligible for benefits in a nursing home that she could not receive living at home. When he realized she wasn't going to a nursing home, he started coming to see her at home, and bringing a nurse along with him. This was unheard of in the 1990s. He also gave me samples of her medications if he had them.

After mother died and I had time to think about my life, it was obvious I could not take up where I left off when I stopped going out and stayed home to take care of my parents. Most of my social contacts were married, deceased or too old to care about going out.

I remained in the house we had lived in since 1961 until I retired October 31, 2000. At that time, I rented the house and moved in with my eldest nephew. After I retired I visited nursing home patients. I started with one and soon I was visiting ten each week. My nephew moved out of state in 2008 and I returned to the house in Hapeville and lived there until I sold it in November of 2011.

I was diagnosed with congestive heart failure in July of 2009 and on my 72nd birthday (October 11, 2011), I had my first atrial fibrillation episode.

I am again living with my nephew in the country about forty miles east of Atlanta. I miss Atlanta and I plan to return soon.

FROM THE 10TH ANNIVERSARY EDITION OF *THE TRANSSEXUAL VOICE*

More than twenty-five years ago, a very courageous Christine Jorgensen brought the world to attention with her sex-change surgery. [Her sex-change surgery was done in Denmark in 1952.]

She is a successful lady; a fine example for us all. However, as the first known transsexual, she is a celebrity and her story does not reflect the true picture of the transsexual's dilemma.

Society has been slow to understand and accept transsexuals. I believe the media is largely responsible; however, we must accept part of the blame.

There are some who call themselves transsexuals who are not. They seem to be the most outspoken and most accessible to the media. These likely are the ones who provide documentation for the incorrect statistics that have been reported by the media. Often the reporter's only interest is getting a story. It doesn't have to be true. They generally label all transsexuals as bizarre and unable to live a successful and useful life.

The bad thing is that the majority of Americans believe that if it appears in the newspapers, it's the truth. They never see any argument because the newspapers do not choose to present the other side; as there is no right of appeal to anything that appears in the newspapers, the public is unaware that a desire to appeal exists.

It is up to you and me to change these statistics. We cannot remain silent and accomplish this. Persons who have thus far had sex-change surgery have the tremendous responsibility of providing society with a correct and believable image.

The way we conduct ourselves now will determine how transsexuals are accepted by society in the future.

AFTERWORD

As you now know, I had sex-change surgery (SRS) in Tijuana, Mexico forty-five years ago on February 6th, 1969. At that time, the surgery was not available in the United States.

Most people with whom I came in contact at that time had never heard of transsexuals, and those who had considered them to be gay or some kind of pervert. Today it would be difficult to find someone who has never known or at least heard of a transsexual. There are many publicly known transsexuals and many more who are not known. The most successful transsexual is an unknown transsexual. They do exist.

It was very difficult to find a surgeon who could and would do sex-change surgery in 1969. I was given the names of two surgeons—Dr. Jesus Barbosa in Tijuana and Dr. Georges Burou in Casablanca, Morocco. I chose Dr. Barbosa because of location.

Not that many years ago, I believed what most people believed—that society was comprised of heterosexuals, gays, bisexuals, transvestites and transsexuals. Today there are so many different labels for different lifestyle choices, I don't even know what some of them mean. In recent years, the term transgender has become a term used to cover most anything you want to be. The following are a few of these designations: Agender, Pangender, Third gender, Two Spirit, Genderqueer and Hijra.

To my knowledge, the word transgender was first used in an article written by a psychiatrist in 1965. Legendary transvestite, Virginia Prince, used the word in her writings. In 1985, I met an attractive, grandmotherly-looking Virginia Prince while at a conference in Anaheim, California. She was seventy-two years old at the time. She died in 2008.

The term transsexualism was first used by a German physician and sexologist Magnum Hirschfield in 1923. And, the first sex-change surgery took place in Germany in 1930. The first sex-change surgery at John Hopkins Hospital in Baltimore, MD was done in 1966, and then discontinued in the late 1960s.

A person considering sex-change surgery should proceed very cautiously. Whatever comfort level you may have in one role might be absent in the other. Once you have visited the operating room, you have forever accepted the result; you cannot retrieve what you have given up. Some women simply have a mastectomy and live happily as a man. If that works for them, then they have made a good choice. That does not mean they have had a sex-change. Sex-change surgery takes place between the legs, not on the chest.

Sex-change surgery is now easily available—perhaps too easily. I'm sure quite a number of individuals have the surgery that should not have it, and others will have it and wish they hadn't. It cannot be reversed.

Society is much more accepting of transsexuals now than in 1969, however, there is still a long way to go. In 2008, a State of Georgia (male-to-female) employee who worked in the General Assembly's Legislative Counsel informed her supervisor of her intentions to begin gender transition. She was later terminated, and reasons given ranged from gender transition being inappropriate to immoral and unnatural. She filed charges and was later reinstated.

I worked for the State of Georgia for thirty years. Seven of those years, I worked across the street from the legislative offices. After working for the state three years, in the fall of 1973, knowledge of my surgery spread rapidly through the state offices. I worked across the street from the capitol, and most of the state office buildings connected with a central cafeteria where I ate lunch every day, and was constantly pointed out.

My last seven years of state employment I worked in a forty-one-story office building located on Peachtree Street at Five Points (a Atlanta landmark). A few months before I retired, I passed two young men in the hall. One of them spoke to me and then turned to the other one and said, "Phoebe is the most famous person in the building." That was thirty-one years after my surgery.

A couple of years earlier, I passed three ladies who were waiting for an elevator. One of them told the other two, "That's a man."

I have never been famous and I was never well known. I was unfavorably known in my world and this was a great hindrance. The only way I could have prevented that was to have cut ties with my family—a step I was not willing to take.

If you are contemplating a sex-change, it will be much easier for you than it was for me because society is much more accepting and surgeons are much easier to locate.

The best advice I could give: Like yourself, love yourself and don't compare yourself to anyone.

Throughout my life, I have never wished to be anyone but who I am. I have never blamed God for my problem and there is no doubt in my mind that God has been with me all the way.

WHY THIS BOOK?

Before I became aware of Christine Jorgensen, I didn't know there was another person in the world like me. I want to leave a record of the way society viewed transsexuals and the difficulties I encountered solving my problem and how slow society has been to understand and accept it.

A society that thinks anyone has the choice of choosing whether or not they are to be born heterosexual, homosexual, transsexual, blind, lame or with any other disability is an uneducated society. No one is one hundred percent anything and that includes normal. If you think you are, do a little research beginning with hormones – estrogen and testosterone – YOU have both of them.

If you think that you don't need to know anything about this subject; you are wrong. Transsexualism is existent to the point that there is no one who is not affected by it. You may not know it, but you know someone who is a transsexual. They may never have sex-change surgery because of family or other reasons, but they will want to. It could be your mate, your parent, your sibling, your child, your friend or even you. Ignorance won't make it go away.

I believe God created the being that I am, and the being that you are; and who and what we are was determined by Him. I believe He is in control of everything – not just some things. The choice was his and He doesn't make mistakes.

I REMIND YOU: I'm not a writer; I have a story that needs to be told and it needs to be told by me. The opinions expressed in this book are strictly my own. I think they are valid.

A WORD OF CAUTION!

BE CAREFUL! OVER TWO HUNDRED TRANSGENDERED PEOPLE WORLDWIDE WERE MURDERED IN 2013. IT CAN HAPPEN ANYWHERE.

With my Best Friend Pebbles – 2003

The cover photo of my father and me was taken on my first birthday, October 11, 1940.

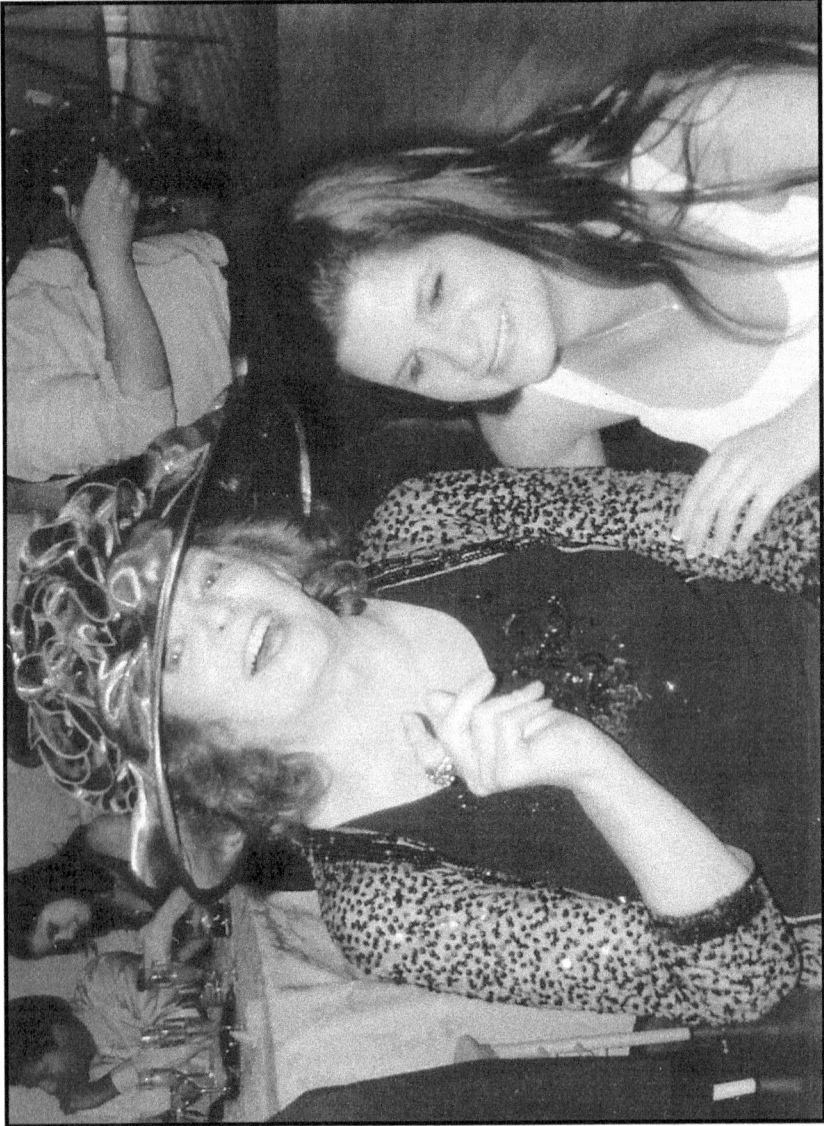

With Cousin Allyson – June 2012